Modern Critical Interpretations

Daniel Defoe's
Moll Flanders

Modern Critical Interpretations

These and other titles in preparation

Modern Critical Interpretations

Daniel Defoe's

Moll Flanders

Edited and with an introduction by

Harold Bloom
Sterling Professor of the Humanities
Yale University

Chelsea House Publishers ◊ *1987*

NEW YORK ◊ NEW HAVEN ◊ PHILADELPHIA

© 1987 by Chelsea House Publishers,
a division of Chelsea House Educational Communications, Inc.,
  95 Madison Avenue, New York, NY 10016
  345 Whitney Avenue, New Haven, CT 06511
  5068B West Chester Pike, Edgemont, PA 19028

Introduction © 1987 by Harold Bloom

Printed and bound in the United States of America

10 9 8 7 6 5 4 3 2 1

∞ The paper used in this publication meets the minimum
requirements of the American National Standard for Permanence
of Paper for Printed Library Materials, Z39.48–1984.

Library of Congress Cataloging-in-Publication Data
Daniel Defoe's Moll Flanders.
  (Modern critical interpretations)
  Bibliography: p.
  Includes index.
  1. Defoe, Daniel, 1661?–1731. Fortunes and
misfortunes of the famous Moll Flanders. I. Bloom,
Harold. II. Series.
PR3404.F653D3 1987   823'.5   87–8029
ISBN 0–87754–947–8 (alk. paper)

Contents

Editor's Note

This book brings together a representative selection of the best criticism devoted to Daniel Defoe's novel *Moll Flanders*. The critical essays are reprinted here in the chronological order of their original publication. I am grateful to Cornelia Pearsall for her aid in editing this volume.

My introduction traces something of the moral perplexities that Defoe represents in Moll Flanders, his most comprehensive fictive character. In a moving account of *Moll Flanders,* Martin Price centers upon Puritan conflicts and self-divisions. John J. Richetti continues the chronological sequence with an essay that contrasts Moll's overt moralizings with the very different purposeful pattern of her actions.

In Miriam Lerenbaum's account of Moll, her "stubborn instinct for self-preservation" is seen as a tribute to her femininity. Maximillian E. Novak pays tribute to Defoe's conscious artistry in the complex narrative of *Moll Flanders,* while Michael M. Boardman emphasizes that "as a creator of human situations, Defoe is far more profound than any of the separate ideas he assigns his characters."

Spontaneity and opportunism are seen by Ian A. Bell as marking both Moll's career as a thief, and as a story-teller rendering her autobiography. Virginia Ogden Birdsall, in a strikingly different analysis, highlights instead Moll's sense of helplessness and her incessant search for authority.

I marvel, as I close this editor's note, at the extraordinary range of these seven essays, which seem to be describing seven different novels, none of them much resembling the one I have sketched in my introduction. This surely suggests the peculiar relevance of Defoe's *Moll Flanders* to the way we live now, since our multiple perspectives diverge much more widely from one another than do most of our contemporary analyses of a canonical novel from our literary past.

Introduction

I

Of his prayers and the like we take no account, since they are a source of
pleasure to him, and he looks upon them as so much recreation.
                              KARL MARX, on Robinson Crusoe

          I got so tired of the very colors!
          One day I dyed a baby goat bright red
          with my berries, just to see
          something a little different.
          And then his mother wouldn't recognize him.
          ELIZABETH BISHOP, "Crusoe in England"

Had Karl Marx written *Robinson Crusoe,* it would have had even more
moral vigor, but at the expense of the image of freedom it still provides for
us. Had Elizabeth Bishop composed it, Defoe's narrative would have been
enhanced as image and as impulse, but at the expense of its Puritan plain-
ness, its persuasive search for some evidences of redemption. Certainly one
of Defoe's novelistic virtues is precisely what Ian Watt and Martin Price
have emphasized it to be; the puzzles of daily moral choice are omnipresent.
Robinson Crusoe and Moll Flanders are human—all-too-human—and suffer what Calvin and Freud alike regarded as the economics of the spirit.

   Defoe comes so early in the development of the modern novel as a
literary form that there is always a temptation to historicize rather than to
read him. But historicisms old and new are poor substitutes for reading, and
I do not find it useful to place *Robinson Crusoe* and *Moll Flanders* in their
contemporary context when I reread them, as I have just done. Ian Watt
usefully remarked that "Defoe's heroes . . . keep us more fully informed of
their present stocks of money and commodities than any other characters in
fiction." I suspect that this had more to do with Defoe than with his age,

1

and that Defoe would have been no less obsessed with economic motives if he had written in the era of Queen Victoria. He was a hard man who had led a hard life: raised as a Dissenter in the London of the Great Plague and the Great Fire; enduring Newgate prison and the pillory in bankrupt middle age; working as a secret agent and a scandalous journalist until imprisoned again for debt and treason. Defoe died old, and so may be accounted a survivor, but he had endured a good share of reality, and his novels reflect that endurance.

Dr. Johnson once said that only three books ought to have been still longer than they were: *Don Quixote, The Pilgrim's Progress,* and *Robinson Crusoe.* Defoe has authentic affinities with Bunyan, but there is nothing quixotic about Robinson Crusoe or Moll Flanders. All of Defoe's protagonists are pragmatic and prudent, because they have to be; there is no play in the world as they know it.

II

With *Robinson Crusoe,* aesthetic judgment seems redundant; the book's status as popular myth is too permanent, and so the critic must ground arms. *Moll Flanders* is another matter and provokes a remarkably wide range of critical response, from the late poet-critic Allen Tate, who once told me it was a great novel of Tolstoyan intensity, to equally qualified readers who deny that it is a novel at all. The overpraisers include James Joyce, who spoke of "the unforgettable harlot Moll Flanders," and William Faulkner, who coupled *Moby-Dick* and *Moll Flanders* as works he would like to have written (together with one of Milne's Pooh books!). Rereading *Moll Flanders* leaves me a touch baffled, as I thought it had been better, it being one of those books that are much more vivid in parts than as a unit, so that the memory holds on to episodes and to impressions, investing them with an aura that much of the narrative does not possess. The status of the narrative is curiously wavering; one is not always certain one is reading a novel rather than a colorful tract of the Puritan persuasion. Moll is a formidable person who sustains our interest and our good will. But the story she tells seems alternately formed and formless, and frequently confuses the rival authorities of fiction and supposed fact.

Martin Price notes how little thematic unity Defoe imposes upon the stuff of existence that constitutes *Moll Flanders.* As a man who had suffered Newgate, Defoe gives us only one key indication of his novel's vision; Moll was born in Newgate and will do anything to avoid ending there. The quest for cash is simply her equivalent of Crusoe's literal quest to survive physically upon his island, except that Moll is more imaginative than the strangely compulsive Crusoe. He does only what he must, she does more, and we begin to see that her obsession has in it an actual taste for adventures. This taste surprises her, but then, as Price observes, she is always "surprised by herself and with herself." She learns by what she does, and almost every-thing she does is marked by gusto. Her vehemence is her most winning quality, but most of her qualities are attractive. Male readers are charmed by her, particularly male readers who both exalt and debase women, among whom Joyce and Faulkner remain the most prominent.

Puritan force, the drive for the soul's exuberant self-recognition, is as much exemplified by Moll as by Bunyan's protagonist. I suspect that was why William Hazlitt, the greatest literary critic to emerge from the tradition of Protestant Dissent, had so violent a negative reaction to *Moll Flanders,* which otherwise I would have expected him to admire. But, on some level, he evidently felt that she was a great discredit to Puritan sensibility. Charles Lamb greatly esteemed her and understood how authentic the Puritan di-alectic was in her, pointing to "the intervening flashes of religious visitation upon the rude and uninstructed soul" and judging this to "come near to the tenderness of Bunyan." Infuriated, Hazlitt responded, "Mr. Lamb admires *Moll Flanders;* would he marry Moll Flanders?" to which the only response a loyal Hazlittian could make is: "Would that Hazlitt had married a Moll Flanders, and been happy for once in a relationship with a woman." All proportion abandoned Hazlitt when he wrote about *Moll Flanders:*

> We . . . may, nevertheless, add, for the satisfaction of the in-quisitive reader, that *Moll Flanders* is utterly vile and detestable: Mrs. Flanders was evidently born in sin. The best parts are the account of her childhood, which is pretty and affecting; the fluctuation of her feelings between remorse and hardened im-penitence in Newgate; and the incident of her leading off the horse from the inn-door, though she had no place to put it in after she had stolen it. This was carrying the love of thieving to an *ideal* pitch and making it perfectly disinterested and mechan-ical.

Hazlitt did not understand Moll, because he could not bear to see the Puritan impulse displaced into "carrying the love of thieving to an *ideal* pitch." Brilliant as the horse-stealing is, it is surpassed by Moll's famous second theft, the episode of the child's necklace:

> Had I gone on here I had perhaps been a true Penitent; but I had an evil Counsellor within, and he was continually prompting me to relieve my self by the worst means; so one Evening he

tempted me again by the same wicked Impulse that had said, *take that Bundle,* to go out again and seek for what might happen.

I went out now by Day-light, and wandred about I knew not whither, and in search of I knew not what, when the Devil put a Snare in my way of a dreadful Nature indeed, and such a one as I have never had before or since; going thro' *Aldersgate-street* there was a pretty little Child had been at a Dancing-School, and was going home, all alone, and my Prompter, like a true Devil, set me upon this innocent Creature; I talk'd to it, and it prattl'd to me again, and I took it by the Hand and led it a long till I came to a pav'd Alley that goes into *Bartholomew Close,* and I led it in there; the Child said that was not its way home; I said, yes, my Dear it is, I'll show you the way home; the Child had a little Necklace on of Gold Beads, and I had my Eye upon that, and in the dark of the Alley I stoop'd, pretending to mend the Child's Clog that was loose, and took off her Necklace and the Child never felt it, and so led the Child on again: Here, I say, the Devil put me upon killing the Child in the dark Alley, that it might not Cry; but the very thought frighted me so that I was ready to drop down, but I turn'd the Child about and bade it go back again, for that was not its way home: the Child said so she would, and I went thro' into *Bartholomew Close,* and then turn'd round to another Passage that goes into *Long-lane,* so away into *Charterhouse-Yard* and out into *St. John's-street,* then crossing into *Smithfield,* went down *Chick-lane* and into *Field-lane* to *Holbourn-bridge,* when mixing with the Crowd of People usually passing there, it was not possible to have been found out; and thus I enterpriz'd my second Sally into the World.

The thoughts of this Booty put out all the thoughts of the first, and the Reflections I had made wore quickly off; Poverty, as I have said, harden'd my Heart, and my own Necessities made me regardless of any thing: The last Affair left no great Concern upon me, for as I did the poor Child no harm, I only said to my self, I had given the Parents a just Reproof for their Negligence in leaving the poor little Lamb to come home by it self, and it would teach them to take more Care of it another time.

This String of Beads was worth about Twelve or Fourteen Pounds; I suppose it might have been formerly the Mother's, for it was too big for the Child's wear, but that, perhaps, the Vanity of the Mother to have her Child look Fine at the Dancing School, had made her let the Child wear it; and no doubt the Child had a Maid sent to take care of it, but she, like a careless Jade, was taken up perhaps with some Fellow that had met her by the way, and so the poor Baby wandred till it fell into my Hands.

However, I did the Child no harm; I did not so much as fright it, for I had a great many tender Thoughts about me yet, and did nothing but what, as I may say, meer Necessity drove me to.

The remarkable moment, which horrifies us and must have scandalized Hazlitt, is when Moll says, "the Devil put me upon killing the Child in the dark Alley, that it might not Cry; but the very thought frightened me so that I was ready to drop down." We do not believe that Moll will slay the child, but she frightens us, because of her capacity for surprising herself. We are reminded that we do not understand Moll, *because Defoe does not understand her.* That is his novel's most peculiar strength and its most peculiar weakness. Gide's Lafcadio, contemplating his own crime, murmurs that it is not about events that he is curious, but only about himself. That is in the spirit of Defoe's Moll. The Protestant sensibility stands back from itself, and watches the spirits of good and of evil contend for it, with the detachment of a certain estrangement, a certain wonder at the immense energies that God has placed in one's soul.

The Divided Heart

Martin Price

The rise of the novel in the eighteenth century is the triumph of the particular, however we may explain the novel's coming into being. Two major tendencies feed into the central event. The mock-heroic of Cervantes and his followers subjects the heroic image to the punishing presence of the commonplace. And the marvelous is naturalized as the saint's life, the rogue's picaresque career, the pilgrimage of the individual soul, are all enmeshed in the business of daily existence. The heroic may survive its punishment, but it takes on a new form. The allegorical translucency of the saint's life or of the pilgrim's progress may survive to some extent, but saint and pilgrim alike have now become first of all people with familiar names and addresses, with aunts and cousins, and the elaborate costume of a social existence. Saints become Clarissa Harlowes; pilgrims become Robinson Crusoes; and rogues become—instead of the resilient heroes of a hundred escapades—characters disclosed in the long, disorderly memoirs of Moll Flanders.

The triumph of the particular is the triumph of formal realism, a realism used to a different degree and for a different end by each of the great novelists of the century. The novel provides a spacious vehicle, with its slow rhythm of disclosure, its opportunities for dialogue, description, commentary. None of these is new in itself. They appear in epic, in romance, and in the genres of drama—but the mixture is new. The novel allows a rapid alternation between the character's internal thought and his action; between his view of himself and the author's view of him; between the

From *To the Palace of Wisdom: Studies in Order and Energy from Dryden to Blake.*
© 1964 by Martin Price. Southern Illinois University Press, 1964.

intense scrutiny and the panoramic view. The novel gains fluidity by its prosiness. It sacrifices the concentration of poetic language for a new fusion of the poetic and the documentary, and for a more thoroughgoing involvement of the significant in the circumstances where it must find its life and from which it must wrest its values. The novel is the medium in which we can see the spirit of man in its most problematic form—not in lucid contests of principle but (in Lionel Trilling's word) "as it exists in the inescapable conditions which the actual and the trivial make for it" (*The Opposing Self*).

Defoe's novels—written late in a career given over to journalism and pamphleteering—have always been a puzzle to the critic. Defoe draws upon forms of autobiography as far apart as criminals' sensational narratives of their careers and Puritan preachers' records of their transactions with God and the devil, factual narratives of sea discoveries, and pious accounts of miraculous providences. Running through this compound is the troubled conscience of a Puritan tradesman, aware of the frequent conflict between the demands of commercial gain and those of spiritual salvation. It is this troubled conscience that gives his characters their depth. They are tremendously efficient and resourceful in meeting the difficulties of their "trade," and Defoe catches the excitement of their limited but genuine art. But they are also nagged by doubt and a sense of guilt, by an awareness of what they have ignored or put by in their single-minded commitment. These pangs are not, in most cases, very effectual, but they are none the less authentic. Defoe's characters participate, as often as not, in what Iris Murdoch calls the "dialectic of those who habitually succumb to temptation."

In the novels I shall consider Defoe gives us the great myth of the isolated man bringing order out of unfamiliar materials (the first part of *Robinson Crusoe*), the outlawry of a woman whose social isolation makes her a freebooter in the center of London (*Moll Flanders*), and the recovery of a man from the life of crime into which he is plunged as a child (*Colonel Jack*). All these characters aspire to some kind of morality; all have a glimpse of some idea of redemption. Without these aspirations, they would be near successors to the picaresque heroes of countless jestbooks, coming through dangerous scrapes with wily dexterity. If the aspirations had fuller control of their natures, they might become the heirs of those spiritual heroes who find their way at last from the City of Destruction of the Land of Beulah. But their lives remain curiously unresolved and open. As Ian Watt has said, "Defoe presents us with a narrative in which both 'high' and 'low' motives are treated with equal seriousness: the moral continuum of his novels is much closer than was that of any previous fiction to the complex combination of spiritual and material issues which moral choices in daily life customarily involve" (*The Rise of the Novel*).

Defoe remains a puzzle because he imposes little thematic unit on his materials. Usually the writer who is content to give us the shape of the tale itself has a shapely tale to tell; a tale with its own logic, its awakening of tensions and expectations, its mounting repetition, its elaborate devices for forestalling too direct a resolution, and its satisfying—perhaps ingeniously surprising—way of tying all its threads in one great stroke. Such a tale need not leave those gaps in its narrative that are occasions for us to consider its meaning or theme. In Defoe's narratives the inconsistencies are such that we want to find a significant design, yet they hardly accommodate our wish.

Some critics have found consistent irony in a work like *Moll Flanders* by trimming away troublesome details, hardening the central character, and importing a moral stridency Defoe does not invite. Dorothy Van Ghent finds in Moll "the immense and seminal reality of an Earth Mother, progenetrix of the wasteland, sower of our harvests of technological skill, bombs, gadgets, and the platitudes and stereotypes and absurdities of a morality suitable to a wasteland world" (*The English Novel: Form and Function*). This seems to me at once a great deal more fastidious and more vehement than the attitudes that underlie Defoe's conception of his heroine. The fact that Moll measures her success by money does not necessarily mean that money is her only object. Nor does Moll's indifference to the sensuousness and concrete texture of experience make her "monstrously abnormal."

Moll Flanders is the chronicle of a full life-span, told by a woman in her seventieth year with wonder and acceptance. In one sense, she is the product of a Puritan society turned to worldly zeal. Hers is very much the world of the Peachums, and in it Moll is the supreme tradeswoman, always ready to draw up an account, to enter each experience in her ledger as profit or loss, bustling with incredible force in the marketplace of marriage, and finally turning to those bolder and franker forms of competitive enterprise, whoredom and theft. To an extent, she is the embodiment of thrift, good management, and industry. But she is also the perverse and savagely acquisitive outlaw, the once-dedicated servant of the Lord turned to the false worship of wealth, power, success.

Her drive is in part the inevitable quest for security, the island of property that will keep one above the waters of an individualistic, cruelly commercial society. Born in Newgate, left with no resources but her needle, she constantly seeks enough wealth or a wealthy enough husband to free her from the threat of poverty and the temptations of crime. But she finds herself fascinated by the quest itself, by the management of marriages, the danger of thievery. When she has more money than she needs, she is still disguising herself for new crimes, disdaining the humble trade of the seamstress. When she finally settles into respectability, it is with a gentleman, not a merchant; her husband is a rather pretentious, somewhat sentimental highwayman, who is not much good as a farmer but is a considerable sportsman. Moll is no simple middle-class mercantile figure; nor is she another Macheath. Yet she has elements of both.

There is still another dimension of Moll Flanders. Her constant moral resolutions, her efforts to reform, her doubts and remorse cannot be discounted as hyposcrisy or even unrealistic self-deception. Moll is a daughter of Puritan thought, and her piety has all the troublesome ambiguities of the Puritan faith. Her religion and morality are not the rational and calculating hyposcrisy of the simple canter—the Shimei of Dryden's *Absalom and Achitophel,* for example. They are essentially emotional. She has scruples against incest, but they take the form of nausea, physical revulsion. She intends virtuous behavior and is astonished to discover her hardness of heart. Moll's life is a career of self-discovery, of "herself surprised," surprised by herself and with herself. Just as for the earlier Puritan, the coming of grace might be unpredictable, terrifyingly sudden, and very possibly deceptive, so for Moll the ways of her heart are revealed to her by her conduct more than by her consciousness, and even her most earnest repentance arouses her own distrust until it can well up into an uncontrollable joy. Personality is not something created or earned; the self is not the stable essence the Stoic moralist might seek. It is something given, whether by God or the devil, always in process, eluding definition and slipping away from rational purpose. Even at her happiest, with the man she has long missed, and in the late autumn of her life, Moll can think of how pleasant life might still be without him. It is a wayward thought, a momentary inclination, as real as her devotion and no more real.

What we find in Moll Flanders is not an object lesson in Puritan avarice or in the misuse of divinely given talents. Moll has all the confusion of a life torn between worldliness and devotion, but what remains constant is the energy of life itself, the exuberant innocence that never learns from experience and meets each new event with surprise and force. Moll, like the secularized puritanism she bespeaks, has the zeal that might found sects as well as amass booty, that might colonize a new world as readily as it robbed an old one. And the form of the old zeal, now turned into a secular world, needing the old faith at least intermittently as the new devotion to the world falters with failure, gives us a pattern of character that is one of the remarkable creations of fiction. Defoe, we are told, seems not to judge his material; Defoe must be a brilliant ironist. Both assertions imply a set of values thinner and more neatly ordered than Defoe can offer. He is aware of the tension between the adventurous spirit and the old piety; he can see the vitality of both religous zeal and worldly industry; the thrifty efficiency and the reckless outlawry that are both aspects of the middle-class adventure; the wonderful excitement of technology as well as its darker omens. And seeing all of this, he does not seem to see the need to reduce these tensions to a moral judgment. Like Mandeville, who struts much more in the role, he is one of the artists who make our moral judgments more difficult.

Ultimately, one might call Defoe a comic artist. The structure of *Moll Flanders* itself defies resolution. In giving us the life-span, with its eager thrust from one experience to the next, Defoe robs life of its climactic structure. Does Moll face marriage to the brother of her seducer, a seducer she still loves? It is an impossible tragic dilemma. Yet the marriage takes place, the husband dies, the children are placed; and Moll is left taking stock as she enters the marriage market again. Does she face the dreadful fact of incest? This, too, passes away; she cannot reconcile herself to it, but she can make a settlement and depart in search of a new and illegal marriage. The commonplace inevitably recurs; we have parodies of tragic situations.

Moll herself is not contemptible in her insensitivity. She is magnificently unheroic; and yet there is a modest touch of heroism in her power of recuperation, her capacity for survival with decency. In her curiously meaningless life, there is a wonderful intensity of experience at a level where affection, inclination, impulse (both generous and cruel) generate all the motions that are usually governed, or perhaps simply accompanied, by a world of thought. We have Defoe's own account of this process in his *Serious Reflections of Robinson Crusoe:*

> There is an inconsiderate temper which reigns in our minds, that hurries us down the stream of our affections by a kind of involuntary agency, and makes us do a thousand things, in the doing of which we propose nothing to ourselves but an immediate subjection to our will, that is to say, our passion, even without the concurrence of our understandings, and of which we can give very little account after 'tis done.

This way of reading *Moll Flanders* imposes its own straitening on the untidy fullness of the book. Ian Watt has made a decisive case for the comparative artlessness of Defoe; there are too many wasted emphases, too many simple deficiencies of realization, to make the case for deliberate irony tenable. But one can claim for Defoe a sensibility that admits more than it can fully articulate, that is particularly alert to unresolved paradoxes in human behavior. Watt dismisses in passing the parallel of a work like Joyce

Cary's *Herself Surprised*. There is point in this dismissal, for Cary has raised to clear thematic emphasis what is left more reticent in Defoe. Yet the relationship is worth exploration. Few writers have been so fascinated as Cary with the ambiguities of the Protestant temper. In a great many characters—among them the statesman, Chester Nimmo in the political trilogy and the evangelical faith-healer Preedy in the last novel, *The Captive and the Free*—Cary studied the shimmering iridescence with which motives seem, from different angles, dedicated service and the search for grace or the most opportunistic self-seeking. Cary was not interested in "rationalization" but in the peculiar power achieved by the coincidence of religous zeal and imperious egoism. Preedy, for example, seduces a young girl and makes her virtually his slave; but he is convinced that his power to win her love is a sign of grace—that a love so undemanding and undeserved as hers can only be a sign of God's love in turn. Preedy is monstrous in one aspect, terrifying but comprehensible in another; the difference lies in what we recognize to be his object.

Cary's effects are so adroit and so carefully repeated that we have no doubt about calling them ironic. Defoe's are less artful and less completely the point of his tale. Yet his awareness of them seems no less genuine. Defoe's characters have secularized old Puritan modes of thought. Moll Flanders is constantly taking inventory and casting up her accounts as she faces a new stage of her life. Crusoe, too, keeps an account book, and, more like the earlier Puritans, an account book of the soul. The doctrine of regeneration, we are told, caused the Puritans "to become experts in psychological dissection and connoisseurs of moods before it made them moralists. It forced them into solitude and meditation by requiring them continually to cast up their accounts" (Perry Miller, *The New England Mind*). In the diary, particularly, the Puritan might weigh each night what he had experienced of God's deliverance or of Satan's temptation during the day. "It was of the very essence of Puritan self-discipline that whatsoever thoughts and actions the old Adam within had most desire to keep hidden, the very worst abominations of the heart, one must when one retired to one's private chamber at night draw into the light bed of conscience. . . . Having thus balanced his spiritual books, he could go to bed with a good conscience, sleep sound and wake with courage" (William Haller, *The Rise of Puritanism*).

The "other-worldliness" of Puritan theology was, as Perry Miller puts it, "a recognition of the world, an awareness of a trait in human nature, a witness to the devious ways in which men can pervert the fruits of the earth and the creatures of the world and cause them to minister to their vices.

Puritanism found the natural man invariably running into excess or intemperance, and saw in such abuses an affront to God, who had made all things to be used according to their natures. Puritanism condemned not natural passions but inordinate passions."

This concern with the uses of things places emphasis not on their sensuous fullness but on their moral function, and the seeming bleakness of Defoe's world of measurables derives in part from this. Characteristically, when Defoe in his *Tour* praises the countryside, it is for what man has made of it: "Nothing can be more beautiful; here is a plain and pleasant country, a rich fertile soil, cultivated and enclosed to the utmost perfection of husbandry, then bespangled with villages; those villages filled with these houses, and the houses surrounded with gardens, walks, vistas, avenues, representing all the beauties of buldings, and all the pleasures of planting." So, too, the natural scene of Crusoe's island "appeals not for adoration, but for exploitation" (Watt). It is not the things we care about but the motives or energies they bring into play: they may satisfy needs, or call forth technical ingenuity, or present temptations. The physical reality of sensual temptation need not be dwelt upon, for moral obliviousness or self-deception is Defoe's concern (as in the account of Moll's going to bed with the Bath gentleman). If Moll's inventories seem gross, they may also be seen as the balance of freedom against necessity; poverty is the inescapable temptation to crime. And her inventories are, in an oblique sense, still account books of the spirit.

What might once have served the cause of piety becomes a temptation to exploitation. This is the dialectic of which Perry Miller speaks: the natural passion insensibly turns into the inordinate passion. Each of Defoe's central characters at some point passes the boundary between need and acquisitiveness, between the search for subsistence and the love of outlawry. And it is only in the coolness of retrospect that they can see the transgression. Defoe does not play satirically upon their defections; he knows these to be inevitable, terrifying so long as they can be seen with moral clarity, but hard to keep in such clear focus. His characters live in a moral twilight, and this leads to Defoe as a writer of comedy.

We must also keep in mind the essential optimism of the Puritan creed. The Puritans could not, Perry Miller tells us, sustain the tragic sense of life. "They remembered their cosmic optimism in the midst of anguish, and they were too busy waging war against sin, too intoxicated with the exultation of the conflict to find occasional reversals, however costly, any cause for deep discouragement. . . . Far from making for tragedy, the necessity [for battle] produced exhilaration." The battle against sin is not, of course, the only battle in which Defoe's characters are involved, but the struggle in the world demands the same intense concentration and affords the same exhilaration. If there is any central motive in Defoe's novels, it is the pleasure in technical mastery: the fascination with how things get done, how Crusoe makes an earthenware pot or Moll Flanders dexterously makes off with a watch. The intensity of this concentration gives an almost allegorical cast to the operation, as if Crusoe's craftsmanship had the urgency of the art by which a man shapes his own soul. It is beside the point to complain that these operations are "merely" technical and practical; undoubtedly the man who invented the wheel had beside him a high-minded friend who reproached him with profaning the mystery of the circle by putting it to such menial uses. The delight in mastery and in problem-solving may be a lower and less liberal art than those we commonly admire, but it is a fundamental experience of men and a precious one.

Even more, the energy of spirit that is concentrated in these operations is a source of joy. One might wish that Moll Flanders had founded a garden suburb with the force she gave to robbing a child, and at moments she feels so too; but the strength she brings to the demands of life is at worst a perversion of the spiritual energy the Puritan seeks to keep alive. It is in doing that he finds himself and serves himself, and Moll Flanders reaches the lowest point of her life when she falls into the apathy of despair in Newgate: "I degenerated into stone, I turned first stupid and senseless, then brutish and thoughtless, and at last raving mad as any of them were; in short, I became as naturally pleased and easy with the place as if indeed I had been born there." She loses her sense of remorse:

> a certain strange lethargy of soul possessed me; I had no trouble, no apprehensions, no sorrow about me, the first surprise, was gone. . . . my senses, my reason, nay, my conscience, were all asleep.

In contrast is the recovered energy that comes with her repentance:

> I was covered with shame and tears for things past, and yet had at the same time a secret surprising joy at the prospect of being a true penitent . . . and so swift did thought circulate, and so high did the impressions they had made upon me run, that I thought I could freely have gone out that minute to execution, without any uneasiness at all, casting my soul entirely into the arms of infinite mercy as a penitent.

These moments of spiritual despair and joy have their counterparts in her secular life as well. After the death of her honest husband, she is left in poverty:

> I lived two years in this dismal condition, wasting that little I had, weeping continually over my dismal circumstances, and as it were only bleeding to death, without the least hope or prospect of help.

With the pressure of poverty and the temptation of the devil, she commits her first theft and runs through a tortured circuit of streets:

> I felt not the ground I stepped on, and the farther I was out of danger, the faster I went. . . . I rested me a little and went on; my blood was all in a fire, my heart beat as if I was in a sudden fright: in short, I was under such a surprise that I knew not whither I was going, or what to do.

This is the energy of fear, but it is a return to life; and before many pages have passed, Moll is speaking with pleasure of her new art.

The benign form of this energy is that of the honest tradesman whom Defoe always celebrates: "full of vigor, full of vitality, always striving and bustling, never idle, never sottish; his head and his heart are employed; he moves with a kind of velocity unknown to other men" (*Complete English Tradesman*). As R. H. Tawney has written, "a creed which transformed the acquisition of wealth from a drudgery or a temptation into a moral duty was the milk of lions" (*Religion and the Rise of Capitalism*). Yet, as Tawney recognizes, the older Puritan view of the evil of inordinate desires still survived, Defoe may call gain "the tradesman's life, the essence of his being" (*CET*), but gain makes it all the harder for a tradesman to be an honest man: "There are more snares, more obstructions in his way, and more allurements to him to turn knave, than in any employment . . . [For] as getting money by all possible (fair) methods is his proper business, and what he opens his shop for . . . 'tis not the easiest thing in the world to distinguish between fair and foul, when 'tis against himself" (*CET*). This candid recognition of the traps of self-deception leads Defoe to a considerable degree of tolerance. He cites the golden rule, "a perfect and unexceptionable rule" which "will hold for an unalterable law as long as there is a tradesman left in the world." But, he goes on, "it may be said, indeed, where is the man that acts thus? Where is the man whose spotless integrity reaches it?" He offers those tradesmen who "if they slip, are the first to reproach themselves with it; repent and re-assume their upright conduct; the general tenor of whose lives is to be honest and to do fair things. And this," he concludes, "is what we may be allowed to call *an honest man;* for as to perfection, we are not looking for it in life" (*CET*).

More fundamental is the "paradox of trade and morality" that Defoe recognizes as well as Mandeville: "the nation's prosperity is built on the ruins of the nation's morals"; or, more cogently, "It must be confessed, trade is almost universally founded upon crime." By this Defoe means what Mandeville means: "What a poor nation must we have been if we had been a sober, religious, temperate nation? . . . The wealth of the country is raised by its wickedness, and if it should be reformed it would be undone" (*CET*). Of luxury, Defoe could write, "However it may be a vice in morals, [it] may at the same time be a virtue in trade" (*The Review*). As Hans H. Anderson (from whose study I have drawn several of these quotations) points out, Defoe does not try to shock his readers as Mandeville does by insisting upon the irreducible paradox; he tends to abstract issues and to exclude "ethical considerations by the simple expedient of restricting his discussion to what he called the 'Language of Trade.' " But, although Defoe does not take pleasure in the difficulties he creates for the moralist, he shows a keen awareness of the difficulties his characters encounter.

Moll Flanders, like Crusoe, is a creature of mixed and unstable motives. She goes to Bath, she tells us, "indeed in the view of taking what might offer; but I must do myself that justice as to protest I meant nothing but in an honest way, nor had any thoughts about me at first that looked the way which afterwards I suffered them to be guided." It is sincere enough, but the moral twilight is clear, too. She lodges in the house of a woman "who, though she did not keep an ill house, yet had none of the best principles in her self." When she has become the mistress of the gentleman she meets at Bath, she remarks that their living together was "the most undesigned thing in the world"; but in the next paragraph she adds: "It is true that from the first hour I began to converse with him I resolved to let him lie with me." The surprise has come in finding that what she had been prepared to accept through economic necessity, she has encouraged through "inclination."

Earlier in America, when Moll discovers that she is married to her brother and the disclosure drives him to attempt suicide, she casts about:

> In this distress I did not know what to do, as his life was apparently declining, and I might perhaps have married again there,

very much to my advantage, had it been my business to have stayed in the country; but my mind was restless too, I hankered after coming to England, and nothing would satisfy me without it.

Here, too, the motives are a wonderful mixture of concern, prudence, and impulse. What is most remarkable about Moll Flanders is her untroubled recognition of her motives, her readiness to set them forth with detachment, at least to the extent that she understands them. She recalls those Puritans who scrutinize their motives as if they were spectators beholding a mighty drama. When Moll robs a poor woman of the few goods that have survived a fire, she records:

> I say, I confess the inhumanity of the action moved me very much, and made me relent exceedingly, and tears stood in my eyes upon that subject. But with all my sense of its being cruel and inhuman, I could never find it in my heart to make any restitution: the reflection wore off, and I quickly forgot the circumstances that attended it.

Fielding was to make something beautifully ironic of this kind of mixture of motives. Defoe uses it differently; candor disarms the moral judgment that irony would require. The stress is more upon the energy of impulse than upon its evil. And the energy is such that it can scarcely be contained by a single motive or be channeled long in a consistent course.

The Dialectic of Power

John J. Richetti

Moll has become in the last forty years or so the most popular of Defoe's characters, at least with critics. The source of that popularity seems to lie in her wonderful inconsistency, a contradiction between the sordid facts of her story and the attractive vitality of her personality. Summing up the matter recently, G. A. Starr has remarked on the ultimate inconsistency: "So if Moll is in some ways the product of sociological and psychological conditioning, in other ways she is quite untouched by experience, a free spirit whom no pitch can defile."

More clearly than his other narratives, *Moll Flanders* allows us to see the precise dynamics of the literary event we are dealing with in reading Defoe's fiction. Strangely enough, to do that we need to remind ourselves that the narrative self in the autobiographical novel is not a person in the ordinary sense and that the events in a narrative do not add up to that cumulative entity emerging from an actual person experiencing the events of a life, which we call "personality" in the domesticated psychoanalytic terms of our time. It should hardly need saying that literary character constitutes a kind of event, a more definable entity than the expanding mystery that "person" implies. The experience we have as we read is of language describing certain events and thereby invoking the special kind of "world" implicit in that language and those events. "Character" is a name we give to the beings who seem to possess that language and promote those events. As Martin Price has said, character in a novel exists within it "as persons in a

From *Defoe's Narratives: Situations and Structures.* © 1975 by Oxford University Press.

society, but the 'society' of the novel is one with intensive and purposive structure." Character, in other words, is most often a means towards expressing the structure of a novel in a way that a person in a society is not a means of expressing the nature of society. Character in fiction tends to mimic the complex of problems implied in the term "personality," but novelistic character is primarily a means towards a large structural end rather than an end in itself.

That notorious contradiction the character of Moll Flanders embodies is the most visible expression of the structure of her novel. Her narrative self is a means of enacting for us independence of the "other," that is, of society, history, and circumstance in general. Novels like Defoe's, of course, pretend to begin with the opposite proposition that the self is precisely defined by the "other" and claim to spend their time showing us just how the self is indeed derived from the other. We have seen, however, that there is a simultaneous push to assert self at the expense of other, that the real movement of Defoe's novels is not simply towards the determinants of character but rather towards the depiction of a dialectic between self and other which has as its end a covert but triumphant assertion of the self. In *Moll Flanders,* that dialectic is at its clearest; the self is visibly apart from the other. This seems a paradoxical state of affairs, for the other is in this case no longer the exotic circumstances and characters which prevail in *Crusoe* or in *Singleton* but what is intended as a version of the real world of bourgeois society. But perhaps the values of personal freedom and individual consciousness that bourgeois culture values most are most possible in the exotic spaces Crusoe and Singleton inhabit and are most endangered in the actual streets of eighteenth-century England. Therefore, if Moll is to be free and really to live in those streets she must, it seems, embody or enact a contradiction which is more than merely lifelike inconsistency.

In truth, the narrative (Moll, if you will, or Defoe) seems aware of that separation and contradiction and strains noticeably towards a rudimentary kind of naturalism. The "editor" claims in the preface that Moll's language has been changed and made fit to be seen and read, that some parts have been omitted, others shortened. Such a claim invites readers to imagine forbidden details, to flesh out the almost austere and rapid sequence that the book really is. But the preface also claims thereby that Moll is the creature of her environment, that her language and point of view coincide with the circumstances she has passed through. An editor is required to separate Moll from her life, to create a Moll who can speak about her life without being what her life implies.

Moll herself begins her story by speculating in her opening paragraphs about what would have become of her under different social circumstances, in a more rational and humane society. There she would have been placed in an orphanage and not "brought into a Course of Life, which was not only scandalous in itself, but which in its ordinary Course, tended to the swift Destruction both of Soul and Body." Moll's theory has little connection with the plain facts of her narrative, for what she experiences by being born in Newgate and passing through various hands until she reaches her "nurse" in Colchester is quickly summarized in several paragraphs and has nothing essentially to do with her subsequent career as a criminal. The facts are that she could as easily have come to her criminal career through any number of alternative sets of circumstances which are not related to the lack of state provisions for orphans and deserted children. Real eighteenth-century criminals were indeed products of vicious circumstances and partly produced by state indifference to child welfare. But Moll, unlike Bob Singleton and Colonel Jack, is not really served badly by the social circumstances surrounding her childhood.

She has sufficient dramatic sense, however, to arrange the opening pages of her narrative in sequences which favour calamity, or often dwell first and foremost upon the melodramatic possibilities of a situation. When her nurse dies, Moll lingers over her childish terrors and the cruel taunts of her nurse's daughter, who withholds her "fortune" of twenty-two shillings: "Now was I a poor Gentlewoman indeed, and I was just that very Night to be turn'd into the wide World; for the Daughter remov'd all the Goods, and I had not so much as a Lodging to go to, or a bit of Bread to Eat." It is only after this scene has been properly elaborated that we are told much more briefly that compassionate neighbours inform the mayoress who had previously taken a fancy to little Moll and she is taken into her household. She becomes, in effect, an upper-servant in that house, raised on a par with the daughters. Not only circumstances but nature, too, joins in all this generosity, as Moll tells us in her summary of her education as a young lady in a gentle house in Colchester: "By this Means I had . . . all the Advantages of Education that I could have had, if I had been as much a Gentlewoman as they were, with whom I liv'd, and in some things, I had the Advantage of my Ladies, tho' they were my Superiors; but they were all the Gifts of Nature, and which all their Fortunes could not furnish."

It is, of course, true that Moll begins as an isolated infant waif. Normally, we would expect that early isolation such as Moll provides for herself would produce insecurity and dependence in adolescence and maturity. But the book cares very little for plausibility of that narrowly personal sort. Moll tries, in a sense, to look both ways in describing her childhood as part of the chain of circumstances which made her what she became. But both the incidents from her childhood that she places before us are as much illustrations of her independence and somehow instinctive sense of strong isolation as they are examples of social determinism. The first of these is a half recollection of being left in Colchester by gipsies when she was a little more than three years old, or perhaps, Moll adds significantly, of her leaving them: "I have a Notion in my Head, that I left them there, (that is, that I hid myself and wou'd not go any further with them)." The natural limitations of recollection require that such precocious independence remain uncertain. Not so the second childhood incident, which is actually the main anecdote that Moll has for us about her early years. Plying her needle, little Moll declares to her nurse that she will never go into service and will live on her own, supporting herself by her spinning and thereby becoming a "gentlewoman." Little Moll innocently supposes that gentle-folk live by their own exertions, that they are independent wage-earners. The reality of gentility is quite the opposite: "all I understood by being a Gentlewoman, was to be able to Work for myself, and get enough to keep me without that terrible Bug-bear *going to Service*, whereas they meant to live Great, Rich, and High, and I know not what." Moll's fantasy is of authentic independence through labour, an apparently rare possibility for very young children who were engaged in spinning yarn for the manufacture of woollens. What Moll will have to learn to do in the course of her narrative is to relinquish this middle-class dream of honest and self-sufficient survival.

In reality, the dream would be quickly dispelled; a worker like Moll, owning nothing but her own ability to work, is a prisoner of the compulsive cycles of the free market. Moll is given this fantasy by the narrative to demonstrate her membership in a category beyond class and real social experience. Her desire to be nothing but her own woman marks her for us readers as an instinctively free spirit, one not bound by inner compulsions like Robinson Crusoe nor committed like Bob Singleton to his own freefloating nullity but aggressively eager to be independent of circumstances from the very start. The problem is that Moll will have to exchange this ideology of personal freedom for the praxis of independence: movement, secrecy, capital accumulation, and constant manipulation of others by constant withholding of the self. It must seem as if in making this exchange, Moll retains her desire for original freedom, a blameless and intact selfhood which is existentially prior to the various false selves forced upon her by social circumstances. The narrative as we read it is a detailed recording of the many forms of social survival, techniques as liberating for the reader as the spectacular survivals of Crusoe and Singleton. But Moll's initial fantasy is crucial in this regard, for it establishes her as a victim who learns to act in self-defence; it posits the pre-social innocence required to face socially imposed necessity with a full ruthlessness which the reader is invited to accept because of the clear moral antithesis involved. That is, Moll's "character" as an event in which we participate is the giving up of the ideology of freedom for the praxis of independence. We participate joyfully in that praxis not simply for its own sweet sake but because we respond to the ideology of personal freedom which supports it and for the loss of which it is the only just recompense.

Moll is taken up into the middle classes by her adolescence in the Mayor's house at Colchester, but she remains outside the middle-class values which that house exemplifies in its residents largely by virtue of her preliminary rooting in freedom. When she is courted and seduced by the "elder brother" of the house, she is committed to a version of the freedom she expressed in her childish wish for self-sufficiency. For in that seduction she is still a victim of nature, that is, of the sense of power provided by her own natural accomplishments and beauty, the mature equivalents of her childish independence. But like that fantasy, Moll's self-confidence is bound for failure by social realities: her education and her natural parts combine to make her an untenable rival for the genuine daughters of the house. Just as circumstances (the death of her nurse) intervene to make her childish independence lapse rather than fail, so here circumstances (the seduction by the elder brother) intervene to divert Moll from actually trying to rise by sheer natural abilities into the middle-class world of her employers. She begins not only as the victim of "nature" but as the sole embodiment of it in the context of the socially established moral cynicism of the household.

This is not to say that the incident is melodrama, that it consists of a simple heroic opposition between nature and society, innocent Moll versus a corrupt and knowing world. Moll does invoke socio-historical conditions and her own ignorance as the specific causes of her seduction: "knowing nothing of the Wickedness of the times, I had not one Thought of my own Safety, or of my Vertue about me." Her seducer, in the same vein, is "a gay Gentleman that knew the Town as well as the Country" and who engineers the seduction by a number of carefully executed stratagems. Moreover, Moll has to claim that her seduction was her original disaster, the source or seed of her ultimate moral degeneration into swindler and criminal. As we read, we are conscious of the whole episode as something rather different, something which happens as much from Moll's sense of freedom as from ignorance, and something which is the real beginning of her strength rather than merely the first surrender to circumstances.

The episode illustrates the characteristic double view of the book towards its incidents. Moll is essentially an active intelligence which transforms itself to meet the needs of experience, but she is also necessarily first a passive entity to whom things happen. The book is aggressively committed like all Defoe's narratives to "variety," to movement of the self through many circumstances and changes. But since those necessary changes must come from the outside, Moll throughout waits for things to happen to her; like Crusoe and Singleton and the others, she depends upon a guaranteed world of whirling circumstances. Even as a thief, for example, she avoids aggressive crimes like house-breaking and counterfeiting. Rather, she walks the streets and waits for the profitable opportunities that will offer themselves. Moll responds to events and dominates them, but she cannot be said to initiate them. What she must have of a primary and assertive nature is a residual self somewhere beneath the various social selves, that authentic self we have already observed in the process of being frustrated and submerged because of the nature of the social world. In meeting hostile circumstances she negates that self, but that negation becomes an affirmation in the process. Some Hegelian terms are, I think, appropriate and illuminating here, for Moll's relationship as self to the "other" of experience is manifestly a dialectical one. In order to "become herself," Moll has to confront the negativity of the other. The two initial terms, the assertive self and the negating other, produce a third term wherein "the first term [self] is found again, only richer and more determinate, together with the second term [other], whose determination has been added to the first determination. The third term [self involved in other] turns back to the first term by negating the second one, by negating therefore the negation and limitation of the first term. It releases the content of the first term, by removing from it that whereby it was incomplete, limited and destined to be negated, or that whereby it was itself negative."

The seduction operates, to translate these terms into the concrete events of the novel, as a rite of passage into the world of sexual and social exploitation that is nothing less than the actual and operative world of the story. But that world is thereby defined as an environment that must be faced and mastered rather than as a set of circumstances that determines the self. The initiate, in this case, remains apart from the world into which she is introduced; the seduction is there precisely to illustrate the necessity of a new knowledge of self as both in and out of the circumstances of its world. The seduction (the second term, the other) releases the self from the negative determination and limitation which define it by itself. Let us call that negatively spontaneous desire.

Young Moll is in this sequence clearly possessed by her own spontaneous desire for what she calls the "person" of her seducer and for the gold he gives her. She describes herself as "taken up Onely with Pride of my Beauty, and of being belov'd by such a Gentleman; as for the Gold I spent whole Hours in looking upon it; I told the Guineas over and over a thousand times a Day." She enacts the compulsive ignorance of self when it naïvely desires the other, since it depends totally upon the other for its fulfilment. In the seduction, Moll is obliterated by the experience: "My Colour came, and went, at the Sight of the Purse, and with the fire of his Proposal together; so that I could not say a Word, and he easily perceiv'd it; so putting the Purse into my Bosom, I made no more Resistance to him, but let him do just what he pleas'd; and as often as he pleas'd; and thus I finish'd my own Destruction at once."

Old Moll's description of the events leading to the seduction reveal the qualities of mind and the self-positioning skill that she is to acquire later, a mind extraordinarily aware of contingencies and always ready to approach experience as a network of possibilities, and always therefore able to stand apart from mere spontaneous experience. Her summary of the situation begins as a moral warning to unwary young women but turns away from such banalities and into the first extended exemplification in the narrative of the amoral analysis of action that defines the style and self of the mature Moll:

> Thus I gave up myself to readiness of being ruined without the least concern, and am a fair *Memento* to all young Women, whose Vanity prevails over their Vertue: Nothing was ever so stupid on both Sides, had I acted as became me, and resisted as Vertue and Honour requir'd, this Gentleman had either Desisted his Attacks, finding no room to expect the Accomplishment of his Design, or had made fair, and honourable Proposals of Marriage; in which Case, whoever had blam'd him, no Body could have blam'd me. In short, if he had known me, and how easy the Trifle he aim'd at, was to be had, he would have troubled his Head no farther, but have given me four or five Guineas, and have lain with me the next time he had come at me; and if I had known his Thoughts, and how hard he thought I would be to be gain'd, I might have made my own Terms with him; and if I had not Capitulated for an immediate Marriage, I might for a Maintenance till Marriage, and might have had what I would; for he was already Rich to Excess, besides what he had in Expectation.

Moll is saying without any equivocation that the purpose of a knowledge of self and of the other, moral or psychological, is self-protection, or, better, self-reservation. Spontaneous desire simply reaches out for the object of desire, thinking that it can appropriate the other directly. The seduction is the first step in the dialectic process which converts spontaneous desire into capable self-possession. The analytical Moll who describes the seduction is the third term that results from the collision of self and other, the calculating self able to operate within the other, seeing the old spontaneous part of itself as merely obeying the determination of the other. The other, too, is now viewed in its negative fullness, as itself bound by its own need to be simply the other. The elder brother's shrewdness is superficial, determined by his own sexual duplicity. He fails to realize Moll's innocence and judges her as if she were as self-interested as he is.

G. A. Starr has observed that "Moll's world is one in which things are not good or evil but characteristically good *and yet* evil," and that the imaginative secret of the book is thus a "double vision" which "extends from the structure of individual sentences and paragraphs to the ethos of the book as a whole." Such an analysis is excellent but static in its implications, taking the moralistic surface of the book as its ultimate content. If we look beyond the categories of good and evil and consider the energy that Moll communicates in her expansive career to us as onlookers, we see that there is a third term beyond the double vision that Starr speaks of which exploits the moralistic antithesis of good and evil. In this opening sequence, we are being prepared for a career in which Moll will repeatedly perform her dialectic with the world and emerge with a self intact or, rather, fortified and expanded.

Her seducer's postcoital advice is that she marry his eager younger brother. Moll's reluctance is part of her still intact ideology of naïve freedom; she cannot "think of being a Whore to one Brother, and a Wife to the other." That is, Moll is not yet ready to do what she will do repeatedly throughout the book—reside comfortably within contradiction, play several inconsistent roles at the same time in order to survive. The elder brother's rhetoric, as Moll presents it, is a series of summarizing clauses, extenuating circumstances: "he entreated me to consider seriously of it, assur'd me that it was the only way to Preserve our mutual Affection, that in this Station we might love as Friends, with the utmost Passion, and with a love of Relation untainted, free from our just Reproaches, and free from other Peoples Suspicions; that he should ever acknowledge his happiness owing to me; that he would be Debtor to me as long as he liv'd, and would be paying that Debt as long as he had Breath." Moll accompanies his soothing casuistry with her melodramatic alternative to the marriage: "turn'd out to the wide World, a meer cast off Whore, *for it was no less,* and perhaps expos'd as such; with little to provide for myself; with no Friend, no Acquaintance in the whole World, *out of that Town.*" But action in this context is made possible by a third possibility, neither the imposed and specious compromise of loveless marriage nor the imposed extravagance of solitary ruin but the clear perception of the necessity of self-preservation: "I began to see a Danger that I was in, which I had not consider'd of before, and that was of being drop'd by both of them, and left alone in the World to shift for myself." From the Hegelian analogy, we can say that this small shift in emphasis is the assertion of a self which locates itself within the compulsions of the other and remains simultaneously outside those compulsions, aware of itself as determined and thereby freeing itself. In choosing marriage with Robin the younger brother, Moll begins, in a small way to be sure, to choose herself rather than the other.

What is obtrusive about this sequence, both before and after the actual seduction, is its minute observation of circumstances, relationships, possibilities, contingencies. In this, the book reveals its almost obsessive interest in the amplification of those possibilities which precede action. What distinguishes *Moll Flanders* from mere criminal biography of the period and what makes the book a novel in the full modern sense of the term is its tendency towards extended meditation on the nature of action rather than the mere description of action itself. Moll seems to develop and emerge as a character in so far as she is constantly preparing for future action even as she indulges in action itself. She is most fully herself when she keeps something of herself (or her substance, frequently and literally her capital) aside and ready for future possibilities. Of course, the perfection of such techniques involves the drastic revision of what we ordinarily think of as personality; it involves dramatic isolation of those self-conscious aspects of personality which turn it into a role, a way of pure and deliberate acting rather than that mixture of the irresistible and the arranged that we think of as self-consciousness.

This opening sequence is very much a preliminary. Moll's self-assertion is still tentative and held in the context of naïve spontaneity. It is only after her quickly summarized five-year marriage to Robin that Moll claims maturity. Courted by various suitors, she refuses to become involved: "The Case was alter'd with me, I had Money in my Pocket, and had nothing to say to them: I had been trick'd once by *that Cheat call'd* LOVE, but the Game was over; I was resolv'd now to be Married, or Nothing, and to be well Married, or not at all."

Even that claim looks premature in terms of what actually happens to her. Moll seems to be concerned still with spontaneous desire. After all, there she is in London now, a merry widow in lodgings presided over by a draper whose sister is "one of the Madest, Gayest things alive." Moll declares openly that she "lov'd the Company indeed of Men of Mirth and Wit, Men of Gallantry and Figure, and was often entertain'd with such." Because of that unsound inclination, she marries unwisely, her husband a draper but one who aspires to gentility, an "amphibious Creature, this *Land-water-thing*, call'd, *a Gentleman-Tradesman*." But her transition from the naïve spontaneity of the seduction is clearly in process, as she describes herself aware of her circumstances, able to manœuvre with skill but unsure of her own best interest: "I was catch'd in the very Snare, which *as I might say*, I laid for my self; *I say laid for myself*, for I was not Trepan'd I confess, but I betray'd my self." That confession, by virtue of its peculiar insistence and repetition, is an assertion of selfhood and independence, especially in Moll's immediate context of a humiliating seduction and a forced marriage.

But the incident records the emergence of Moll's new and mature self in more subtle ways as well. She is now, noticeably, a secret self within the events of the narrative itself, as much outside her behaviour in her actions as she is in her retrospective narration of them. We become fully aware around this point in our career as readers of the book that Moll's greatest concern as a narrator is to establish her separate consciousness as an actor in the events of her life. Thus, she here observes that she observed then as a widow on the make that "the brightest Men came upon the dullest Errand, *that is to say*, the Dullest, as to what I aim'd at." Moll's control within her narrative is a matter of separateness as actor, a sense of apartness much more consistent than either Crusoe's or Singleton's. Unlike them, moreover, she has already mastered the art of indirect discourse and action, as indeed she is forced to by the much more sophisticated society in which she moves. For example, Moll tells us that she liked men of wit and spirit; that is, she is sexually attracted to men who are socially versatile and thereby, by her own implication and emphasis, sexually potent. That is the meaning of Moll's explanation of her preference for a man "that was something of a Gentleman too; that when my Husband had a mind to carry me to the Court, or to the Play, he might become a Sword, and look as like a Gentleman, as another Man; and not be one that had the mark of his Apron-strings upon his Coat, or the mark of his Hat upon his Periwig; that should look as if he was set on to his Sword, when his Sword was put on to him, and that carried his Trade in his Countenance." The sword is a badge of aristocratic sexuality, a device which accompanies and underlines the sexuality implicit in the kind of social versatility Moll here admires. But, alas, such men are naturally disinclined for the married security Moll also desires. Moll presents herself to these gay pseudo-gentlemen as someone of like mind, but she is also of another mind. She wants, that is, to combine sexuality and social versatility with the stability (sexual and social) of marriage. Her curious reticence to say just that, her coy paradox that makes their single-minded liveliness into "dullness," is of a piece with her complicated and disguised desires.

In marrying her "Gentleman-Tradesman," Moll is doing much more than miscalculating and obeying the social and psychological probabilities of her situation. On the level of structure that character exists to further, she is setting out on the first of many excursions into the social contradiction and inconsistency that the book reveals and tries to master. Moll is herself a contradictory mixture, half waif and child cottage spinner, half middle-class young lady. As a widow of limited substance, she is, like her new husband, involved in aspiring and aggressive social movement. Indeed, the highlight of their marriage, the only incident from it that Moll relates, is their impersonation of nobility during an extravagant jaunt to Oxford. That hilarious trip is the concrete if exaggerated expression of what their marriage represents: social versatility and aspiration. All this underlines the real and recurring structure and function of the book: to enact a self which can move freely through social circumstances, revealing at once their superficiality and their desirability, providing the satisfactions of free social movement by a solid and established self whose consciousness is somehow based beyond social circumstances even while cunningly and joyously moving through them. As everyone knows, *Moll Flanders* is about eighteenth-century social and economic realities, but it is also about the superior reality of a self which moves through them, mastering them with a powerful dialectic rhythm and never succumbing to their full implications as cumulatively limiting realities.

To be sure, the book may be said to reveal and dramatize the difficulty of such an accommodation of reality to the desires of the self. The draper is soon bankrupt and decamps for France, leaving Moll in the position of having "a Husband, and no Husband." This latter is one of Moll's favourite constructions. She tells us that her Bath lover "had a Wife" and that "he had no Wife, that is to say she was as no Wife to him." Her banker's clerk tells her, in the same way, "I have a Wife and no Wife." Moll is herself at Bath "a Woman of Fortune, tho' I was a Woman without a Fortune." Such a construction points not to ambiguity but to contradiction, a total disparity between social appearance and personal reality which is the pervasive condition the narrative dramatizes. Earlier, Moll had been unable to consider being both whore and wife. Now she has learned a strategy to meet contradiction with disguise. The evasive action she learned as a courted widow is now intensified and literalized. She retires to the Mint under the first of many aliases, Mrs. Flanders. There, to borrow her construction, she is a debtor and no debtor.

The Mint, like Newgate later in the story, is distilled social compulsion, a place which exemplifies the inexorability of social determinants. Yet here is Moll, friendless, as she tells us, and in retreat from her husband's creditors, a debtor finding safety in debtors' prison, audaciously converting circumstances into a version of freedom. Her disdain for her fellows in the Mint reveals the quality of her strength; her superiority to them lies, again, in her separation from the facts and her real residence in her self:

> But it is none of my Talent to preach; these Men were too wicked, even for me; there was something horrid and absurd in their way of Sinning, for it was all a Force even upon themselves; they did not only act against Conscience, but against Nature; they put a Rape upon their Temper to drown the Reflections, which their Circumstances continually gave them; and nothing was more easie than to see how Sighs would interrupt their Songs, and paleness, and anguish sit upon their Brows, in spight of the forc'd Smiles they put on; nay, sometimes it would break out at their very Mouths, when they had parted with their Money for a lewd Treat, or a wicked Embrace.

Clearly, what Moll finds contemptible in these men is their lack of control and consistency. Like all of Defoe's characters, she learns to be more horrified by disorder than by evil. We can add that as characters in fiction they are justified in equating disorder and evil, for disorder precludes the order that constitutes being and freedom for a character. The delusive idea of freedom implicit in the dissipations of Moll's degenerate associates in the Mint is escape from circumstances by pleasure, a temporary solipsism that Moll despises as ineffective. She realizes here and in her subsequent actions what Georg Simmel insisted upon, that "freedom is not solipsistic existence but sociological action," and that it is a continuing struggle to escape the domination of particular relationships with others and with institutions. In fact, her career begins to fit the rest of Simmel's analysis of freedom: "But it no less consists in a power relation to others, in the possibility of making oneself count within a given relationship, in the obligation or submission of others, in which alone it finds its value and application."

Indeed, Moll emerges from the Mint as an expert female tactician, now fully accomplished and without even the small illusions she cherished before. She helps a friend trick a reluctant suitor into marriage and from that experience resolves to engineer her own survival. Once again, this involves further disguise and even, in Moll's own terms, outright transformation: "I resolv'd therefore, as to the State of my present Circumstances; that it was absolutely Necessary to change my Station, and make a new Appearance in some other Place where I was not known, and even to pass by another Name if I found Occasion." But she goes further than this. On the advice of the friend she has helped, she resolves to take the offensive, to become a man by adopting the aggressively fraudulent tactics of the male world: "as we had observ'd, *as above,* how the Men made no scruple to set themselves out as Persons meriting a Woman of Fortune, when they had really no Fortune of their own; it was but just to deal with them in their own way, and if it was possible, to Deceive the Deceiver."

But the book is nicely delicate in such crucial matters. Moll never becomes, even later in her worst moments as a thief, a nakedly aggressive character. She retains her theoretical innocence as a character by a series of quasi-legal protective measures and self-reservations. Through a careful series of suggestions, her suitor is led to believe that she is wealthy, and her insistence on her poverty in that context becomes a way of convincing him that she is wealthy. She is, to return to her own construction, a cheat and no cheat:

> Besides, tho' I had jested with him, as he suppos'd it, so often about my poverty, yet, when he found it to be true, he had foreclosed all manner of objection, seeing whether he was in jest or in earnest, he had declar'd he took me without any regard to my Portion, and whether I was in jest or in earnest, I had declar'd my self to be very Poor, so that *in a word,* I had him fast both ways; and tho' he might say afterwards he was cheated, yet he could never say that I had cheated him.

It needs to be emphasized that Moll in this sequence, and indeed from the date of her first widowhood in London, operates with female accomplices. Moll's career is, on the surface, a series of relationships with men, but those relationships are usually subordinate to a powerful and instrumental alliance with a female conspirator. Her career culminates in a relationship with a woman: the "governess" who helps her become a master-thief. Defoe's characters, famous for their individuality, tend to acquire allies at moments of action, characters who help them to act and absorb at the same time most of the blame for action. Moll here marries her Virginia planter and enters the visible social structure of marriage, but the real alliance is with the invisible league of self-conscious women, an informal but powerful organization. Women thus "organized" are, like pirates and traveller-merchants, a society within society, an authentic group manipulating the inauthentic relationships ordinary society offers.

Moll passes directly (in terms of narrative space, a few paragraphs) into another relationship with a woman, this time her mother-in-law/mother in Virginia. The trip itself, by the way, is of no interest to the narrative, summarized in a paragraph in spite of its dreadful storms and encounter with a pirate. What matters for Moll is the powerful alliance with her mother-in-law in the face of complex circumstances, the real dangers that the narrative is interested in. Faced with another contradiction, the greatest one yet, that she is once again a wife and no wife, married to her brother, Moll passes quickly from the rhetoric of desolation to the tactical joys of analysis and self-preservation. Viewed as a character in the normal affective sense, her calm in this crisis is monstrous as well as implausible. But in terms of her real function as an indestructible personal energy centre, her control is appropriate and actually winning. She waits for her mother's "Rhapsodies" to subside and, "When these things were a little over with her we fell into a close Debate about what should be first done before we gave an account of the matter to my Husband." What the women fear and seek to neutralize is the practical power and emotional incompetence of Moll's husband/brother: "we could neither of us see our way thro' it, nor see how it could be safe to open such a Scene to him; it was impossible to make any judgment, or give any guess at what Temper he would receive it in, or what Measures he would take upon it; and if he should have so little Government of himself, as to make it publick, we easily foresaw that it would be the ruin of the whole Family, and expose my Mother and me to the last degree."

So two women, Moll and her mother, share a secret, a characteristic situation in the novel. It can be said that in Defoe's narratives in general the secret is the source of personal authenticity, what sets a character apart from his society, guarantees and sustains that apartness, and in short makes him a character. Criminals like Captain Avery and Moll in her criminal phase are thus always attractive figures in an individualistic culture. Their secret criminality, it can be argued, is primarily a means towards a dramatic apartness and consequently undeniable authenticity rather than a significant act *per se*. The interest and complexity of *Moll Flanders* lie not only in the varieties of apartness, criminal and legal, that it enacts but also in its ability to locate Moll both within and without society, to keep her moving through society and within herself at approximately the same time. To put it another way, the book's greatest achievement in relation to Defoe's narratives is to make her apartness a social necessity and personal reality rather than a fantasy of escape. For Moll's exact secret here in Virginia with her husband/brother is that she is disqualified from social participation and at the same time threatened by a powerful world of legal forms and institutions: "and if at last he should take the Advantage the Law would give him, he might put me away with disdain, and leave me to Sue for the little Portion that I had, and perhaps wast it all in the Suit, and then be a Beggar; the Children would be ruin'd too, having no legal Claim to any of his Effects; and thus I should see him perhaps in the Arms of another Wife in a few Months, and be my self the most miserable Creature alive." The sequence of disasters—legal, financial, personal—reveals the instinctive priorities of Moll's being. It is not, as some have been quick to assume, that she despises the personal, but rather that she enacts in her character and career the fact that the personal depends upon the legal and the financial for its existence. Moll's ultimate secret is not really her incest but her knowledge of that sequence, her knowledge that the individual sustains himself by consciousness of social forms and thereby negates their negation and affirms a new kind of self.

This process of dialectical transformation of disastrous social circumstances into personal affirmation and freedom is actually what occurs. Moll's revelation to her husband/brother is a model of steely control, made all the more formidable by contrast with his near collapse: "I observ'd he became Pensive and Melancholly; and in a Word, as I though a little Distemper'd in his Head; I endeavour'd to talk him into Temper, and to Reason him into a kind of Scheme for our Government in the Affair, and sometimes he would be well, and talk with some Courage about it." But he attempts suicide twice, and Moll finds herself changed by these circumstances: "My pity for him now began to revive that Affection, which at first I really had for him." His despair changes "into a long ling'ring Consumption" and Moll finds herself "restless too, and uneasie; I hanker'd after coming to *England,* and nothing would satisfie me without it." The pattern is clear: Moll submits to circumstance and admits her incest, although her admission is carefully planned and her relationship to the incest is made into an objective one. That negation negates itself in her husband/brother's illness, and Moll is fortified and propelled to England in a new and richer version of herself. The narrative is at pains to be specific about this combination of circumstances and inner desire which transforms Moll: "and so *my own Fate pushing me on,* the way was made clear for me, and *my Mother concurring,* I obtain'd a very good Cargo for my coming to *England.*" That precise alignment of desire and circumstance is what all Defoe's characters strive for, and as such it may be said to mark the end of a division in Moll's career. In returning to London, Moll embarks on a new stage of her life, one in which she is to repeat the relationships she has had so far as mistress and wife but with a new consciousness and a refined skill in the art of survival.

The quality of that consciousness is evident in the way Moll positions herself, having learned the secret of active placement of the self where it can respond to circumstances in a profitable manner. If we listen to Moll's explanations, she seems still to be caught up in spontaneous desire. Bath, she explains, "is a Place of Gallantry enough; Expensive, and full of Snares; I went thither indeed in the view of taking any thing that might offer." But she also explains that she is still caught in contradiction, "being now, *as it were,* a Woman of Fortune, tho' I was a Woman without a Fortune." She is, in fact, waiting (or lying in wait) for opportunity to offer, trusting in a world of bountiful circumstances which the agile self can master and turn to self-advantage: "I expected something, or other might happen in my way, that might mend my Circumstances as had been my Case before." There is a progression at work here. Moll has gone from innocent maiden to gay and partially designing widow, and then to calculating bigamist with her husband/brother after her gentleman-tradesman has run away. There has been a fairly precise increase in each connection of Moll's power in relation to the institution of marriage, that is, her action has acquired increasing sociological meaning. Her personal power is exercised both within the various relationships and in relation to the institution of marriage. And in dominating marriage itself, Moll exercises power over society. She takes the office of mistress and in the process of her narrative converts that initial sexual irregularity (with the elder brother) which makes her totally vulnerable into a liberating and totally dominant position in a parallel relationship with her Bath lover.

That dominance in the context of that pattern is behind the curious relationship she has with her Bath lover, a courtship in which her victory is a matter of almost total reserve. She allows him (again by means of a female accomplice, her landlady) to propose assistance and then refuses it. He offers again: "However, it was not long before he attack'd me again, and told me he found that I was backward to trust him with the Secret of my Circumstances, *which he was sorry for;* assuring me that he enquir'd into it with no design to satisfie his own Curiosity, but meerly to assist me, if there was any occasion." The code is clear enough. If Moll reveals herself and asks for "assistance," she becomes a dependent mistress. So Moll holds out, "secretly very glad," but refusing to ask. She accepts money, however, but in a ritualized way which preserves her independence and makes him the sexual aggressor. He asks her to bring him all her money and then to fetch his money box:

> He took the Drawer, and taking my Hand, made me put it in, and take a whole handful; I was backward at that, but he held my Hand hard in his Hand, and put it into the Drawer, and made me take out as many Guineas almost as I could well take up at once.
>
> When I had done so, he made me put them into my Lap, and took my little Drawer, and pour'd out all my own Money among his, and bad me get me gone, and carry it all Home into my own Chamber.

In spite of the overt sexual suggestions of this gift and its manner, their relationship remains chaste, and that chastity is in context a sign of Moll's power over her lover, since her reserve extracts these elaborate means of self-display from him. At his suggestion, they perform extensive feats of sexual abstinence: "I frequently lay with him, and he with me, and altho' all the familiarities between Man and Wife were common to us, yet he never once offered to go any farther, and he valued himself much upon it." Her lover offers this service as an earnest of his real affection, as something that he supposes will please her and enhance him in her eyes. Like the strange ceremony with the money, it is a ritualized act of service which Moll presents in order to expose its coercive and self-serving nature.

Their chastity ends when Moll allows him "to discharge him of his Engagement for one Night and no more." Moll's confessed wickedness renders this bizarre affair all the more impressive as an expression of her power, since she says she mastered her own spontaneous desire for him up to this point in order to achieve perfect mastery of her lover and the situations he has devised. Psychologically, I think, the incident makes little sense, unless we care to invoke a suddenly complicated reciprocal of desire and repression as the secret of Moll's personality. What we have in her is not an analysand but a character in a narrative context performing certain acts. Those acts in the particular context created by the narrative (a woman of no fortune, technically a bigamist, depending upon a married man for her survival) are an extraordinary assertion of control, a transformation (comic and joyous) of the office of mistress and of the sociological reality of male dominance in such a relationship. The concrete truth of the narrative and the pleasure it seeks to give us as readers lie in such a formulation, somewhat different from the facts of mere personality.

From the beginning of her story, of course, Moll has offered other interpretations of these and other facts of her career. These comments form a kind of moralistic superstructure, sometimes plausible and parallel to the other structure I am concerned with, sometimes not. Here, for example, Moll laments her weakness, her surrender to her Bath lover, but defends it as the result of circumstances and irresistible inclination: "It is true, *and I have confess'd it before,* that from the first hour I began to converse with him, I resolv'd to let him lye with me, if he offer'd it; but it was because I wanted his help and assistance, and I knew no other way of securing him than that: But when we were that Night together, and, as I have said, had gone such a length, I found my Weakness, the Inclination was not to be resisted, but I was oblig'd to yield up all even before he ask'd it." That happens to be, if we check Moll's cross reference, not quite the case. She recorded a very careful set of tactics to extract submission only on her terms; in her chronology, she declares that she would have submitted to him only after he had acknowledged her moral superiority and helped establish her financial independence. Her narrative as we read it says something different from her occasional moralistic summaries. The latter stress dependence upon compulsive circumstances; the narrative proper enacts purposeful action. It is the pattern we noticed at the beginning of this chapter and the characteristic pattern of Defoe's narratives: free action in the context of compelling circumstances.

"A Woman on Her Own Account"

Miriam Lerenbaum

Ian Watt's *Rise of the Novel* has inspired many readers to study *Moll Flanders* with new appreciation, and many critics to engage in what amounts to a pamphlet war on a number of issues Watt has raised. None, though, seems to have given serious consideration to his thoughts on Moll's femininity, or rather her *non*-femininity. Watt writes: "The essence of her character and actions is, to one reader at least, essentially masculine. . . . it is at least certain that Moll accepts none of the disabilities of her sex, and indeed one cannot but feel that Virginia Woolf's admiration for her was largely due to admiration of a heroine who so fully realized one of the ideals of feminism: freedom from any involuntary involvement in the feminine role."

The purpose of this paper is to marshal evidence from the novel itself, from social histories of the period, and from recent biological and psychological writings to suggest that, contrary to Watt's impression, Defoe has given us in *Moll Flanders* an exceptionally accurate rendering of his heroine's "involuntary involvement in the feminine role." Or, as Virginia Woolf puts it, Defoe "makes us understand that Moll Flanders was a woman on her own account and not only material for a succession of adventures."

Such a thesis about *Moll Flanders* would certainly not make the book an anomaly in his writings. In such early short works as the section advocating advanced education for women in *An Essay on Projects* (1697) and the verse-satire *Good Advice to the Ladies* (1702) and in his close examinations of marriage both fictional (*Roxana*, 1724) and nonfictional (*Conjugal Lewdness*,

From *The Authority of Experience: Essays in Feminist Criticism*, edited by Arlyn Diamond and Lee R. Edwards. © 1977 by the University of Massachusetts Press.

1727), Defoe shows that he is an acute observer of women and sympathetic to their plight. Similarly, in *Moll Flanders* he has contrived a narrative in which the major turning points of the heroine's life and her responses to them are in great part peculiarly feminine. Although there is no absolute line to be drawn between a voluntary and involuntary acceptance of the feminine role, there is a wealth of evidence to support the view that Moll's responses and attitudes are intimately tied to the social expectations for and restrictions upon women of her time and place and to the biological processes that continue to affect women of our time and place. Defoe has not fashioned Moll according to a moral model. He has created her out of everyday fact and human psychology, particularly as they relate to the actualities of feminine roles.

In *Moll Flanders*, Defoe takes cognizance of Moll's roles as young woman, wife, mother, thief, and pioneer, most especially by correlating the stages in her aging process with crises in her personal life. He concludes each stage and introduces the next with an episode in which Moll, confronted by a seeming impasse, falls psychosomatically ill, becomes inert and passive for a period of time, and then subsequently recovers to begin a wholly new career with energy and optimism. There are three major instances: the first precedes her matrimonial career; the second comes at its conclusion and introduces her thieving career; the third occurs in Newgate and marks the beginning of her "new life," reunited with her favorite husband and pioneering in the New World. Between the first and second of these major crises, there is an important minor episode of the same kind: she falls ill when she is pregnant and "between husbands." These episodes help to give shape to the narrative and provide a convenient way of organizing a consideration of the essentially feminine nature of Moll's behavior.

Moll and Her Prospects

The first of Moll's three major bouts of illness occurs in the midst of the well-known sequence of scenes describing her affair with the "elder brother" and her subsequent marriage to Robin, the "younger brother." Moll is here between seventeen and eighteen years old. Her report of her illness occupies three paragraphs, the major details of which I quote:

> The bare loss of him as a gallant was not so much my affliction
> as the loss of his person, whom indeed I lov'd to distraction; and
> the loss of all the expectations I had, and which I always built my
> hopes upon, of having him one day for my husband. These

> things oppress'd my mind so much that, in short, the agonies of
> my mind threw me into a high fever, and long it was that none
> in the family expected my life. . . . After the end of five weeks I
> grew better, but was so weak, so alter'd, and recover'd so slow-
> ly, that the physicians apprehended I should go into a consump-
> tion; and which vex'd me most, they gave their opinion that my
> mind was oppress'd, that something troubl'd me, and, in short,
> that I was in love.

From this description we learn that Moll is psychosomatically ill with delir-
ium and high fever, but that she and the doctor only partly concur in
assigning this illness a cause. He calls it love, but she tells us that it was this
and more—that she has also lost all her expectations of marrying well and
marrying for love. Between her first rendezvous and her illness, Moll has
moved from innocence to experience with traumatic consequences.

A number of genuinely depressing truths have impressed themselves
upon her mind during this interval. She learns that despite their mutual
passion, the elder brother will not marry her; that he will not come into his
inheritance for years; that his loyalty to his younger brother exceeds his
devotion to her; that Robin is highly unlikely to gain his family's approval
to marry her; and that willy-nilly she will be cast into the servitude she sees
as a yawning abyss, has stubbornly sought to avoid, and had been misled
into thinking she has completely, if narrowly, escaped. If we are willing to
take Moll's plight seriously, we will see how brilliantly Defoe has depicted
the crisis of a young woman whose whole future life has turned to ashes.

In making our judgment of Moll's own assessment, we must avoid
romanticizing her prospects. Not only Moll, but everyone around her,
thinks the younger brother mad to marry solely for love. Moll herself has
no dowry, no social position, no special assets with which to gain a husband
or earn a decent living. There was a time when English women of all classes
had held important places in the working life of the community, but that
time had passed. One could not make a casual decision to enter those sectors
of the work force that promised a decent wage in a respectable profession,
for apprenticeship and licensing were required for most occupations, and
both Moll's upbringing and society's active discouragement effectively
closed such an alternative—to married women as well as to unmarried ones.

Remaining single is not in any event a real alternative for Moll. Although many men freely chose a single life, both the law and the prac-
ticalities of everyday life treated every woman of the period as married or
about to be. Even such severe critics of marriage as Defoe himself never

suggest that women might validly choose not to be married; their only advice is the kind Defoe proffers: that women choose their husbands with great care. At the outset of her marriage career, Moll is not able to make even this choice. If she has been nourishing a *Pamela*-like fantasy, her inquisition of the elder brother has decisively toppled it.

That Moll does not exaggerate her fears of unattractive and extended servitude if she cannot successfully extricate herself from her impasse is clear from Dorothy George's meticulous account of the fate of most parish children of the period: "there can be no doubt that those [cases] which came into court represent an infinitesimal proportion of the little apprentices who were beaten, starved and neglected, still less of those who ran away to become beggars and vagrants. *Little girls especially were liable to be horribly ill-used. . . .* There were also trades so unprofitable or disagreeable that only parish children or the children of the very poor were apprenticed to them." Although a combination of good luck and fearful stubbornness has so far relieved Moll of the worst possibilities of being a parish child, she is certainly entitled to feel terrified of her possible future fate. Her skill in needlework would only consign her to an even bleaker future than entry into domestic service. Yet if Moll incurs the enmity of her protectors, only these prospects confront her. The elder brother represents Moll's introduction to male complacency as he slickly extricates himself from his vows, speaking of *his* possible "ruin" while appearing "surpriz'd at [Moll's] obstinacy." Moll does not choose her future career; it is thrust upon her by all the forces of society.

Society prepares her ill for the marital career it virtually demands of her. Although we hear few details of Moll's day-to-day married life, we know enough of her early life to draw some conclusions, and it seems clear that she is neither better nor worse than she should be. Pleading for a better education for women, William Law might almost be describing Moll's upbringing and its consequences: "The corruption of the world indulges them in great vanity and mankind seems to consider them in no other view than as so many painted idols, that are to allure and gratify their passions; so that if many women are vain, light gewgaw creatures, they have this to excuse themselves, that they are not only such as their education has made them, but such as the generality of the world allows them to be." If Moll is self-indulgent and wilful, it is because she has been encouraged to be so by those around her. Her orphaned state serves only to sharpen her vulnerability to flattery and praise. The memoir form encourages her to be honest and outspoken about her aspirations, but her wishes and values are themselves neither unconventional nor unfeminine. She does not rebel against the feminine role: Moll assures us that for the duration of each of her marriages she was a good wife and mother, amiable and docile, and we have no reason to disbelieve her. She displays initiative and independence only in picking up and starting again in the one career that is available to her.

In her succession of short-lived marriages Moll is also more representative than we might think. After recounting a number of reports of deaths by starvation in eighteenth-century London, Dorothy George writes: "It is significant that all the victims should have been women; there can be little doubt that the hardships of the age bore with especial weight upon them. Social conditions tended to produce a high proportion of widows, deserted wives, and unmarried mothers, while women's occupations were overstocked, ill-paid and irregular." As if intent on illustrating this extract, Defoe has caused Moll to exemplify all those varieties of abandoned women at one stage or other of her marital career. If she anxiously tallies her assets at the close of each of her marriages, it is not because she is paranoid or obsessively greedy, or a symbol of the capitalist spirit, but because she has a clear and accurate picture of her possible fate. If she is never quite so poor or quite so close to disaster as she imagines, neither is she safe. We should not be surprised that much later in life she finds a beggar's dress (one of her temporary robbing costumes) "ominous and threatening." Moll's society does not grant her the luxury of making Alfred Doolittle's choice to be one of either the deserving or undeserving poor. In Shaw's *Pygmalion,* Doolittle claims that "my needs is as great as the most deserving widow's that ever got money out of six charities in one week for the death of the same husband." But England in Moll's lifetime did not yet boast such charitable societies, and even the indomitable Doolittle hasn't "the nerve for the workhouse."

Although all of Moll's marriages are shortlived, she moves from one to the next with increasing concern but without excessive anxiety. We hear of severe emotional distress only at the opening and close of her marital career. The first of these illnesses is as genuine as the last. More than merely extreme adolescent disappointment or particular vanity and egotism, it is an acknowledgment of the disillusionment experienced by the generality of women in Moll's condition and era. Before the age of twenty, all of Moll's romantic hopes are dashed and all of her options are foreclosed. Her severe illness in the face of this crisis is therefore a plausible and significant emblem of her involvement in the feminine role.

MOLL AS MOTHER

The second illness Moll reports is a minor one; it occurs while she is pregnant with a child whose father is Jemy, her highwayman-husband.

Although it does not mark a turning-point in her life, it is significant in relation to the question of her femininity, and provides a useful starting point for an exploration of her role as a mother.

Moll describes this illness: "In the course of this affair I fell very ill, and my melancholly really encreas'd my distemper; my illness prov'd at length to be only an ague, but my apprehensions were really that I should miscarry; I should not say apprehensions, for indeed I would have been glad to miscarry, but I cou'd never entertain so much as a thought of taking any thing to make me miscarry, I abhorr'd, I say, so much as the thought of it." This episode is really one of a pair. At this point she is looking for a midwife; subsequently she searches for a way to disencumber herself of the newly-born child. It was, she says, an "inexpressible misfortune. . . . to have a child upon my hands," for it will interfere with her plan to marry the banker. Throughout this sequence, she reflects—to herself, her governess, and the reader—upon the difficulties and the responsibilities that child-bearing entails, and these reflections, together with her earlier cavalier attitudes towards her children and her later ecstatic reunion with her son in Virginia, have seemed to many readers the epitome of hypocrisy, immorality, inhumanity, and certainly unfemininity.

It is certainly clear that Moll, presumably (or as Ian Watt would say, "suspiciously") like her creator, displays little interest in her children, even to the point of forgetting their existence once they have left her immediate care. Nor do we hear any thing of them while they remain in her care. However, we cannot on that account convict her of unnatural cruelty, for the weight of historical and psychological evidence suggests that in her maternal role, as in other roles, Moll is at one with her female contemporaries.

Although statistics about the facts of seventeenth- and eighteenth-century motherhood are hard to come by, a number of useful clues to general attitudes and practices are available. Within *Moll Flanders* itself, the strictures against deliberately induced abortion suggest that such a practice cannot have been rare or exotic. Numbers of pregnant women must have sought to avoid parenthood. Some even resorted to infanticide: "If, in the worst years [1720–1750], according to the Bills [of Mortality], over 74 per cent of the children born in London died before they were five, parish children, that is, children in workhouses, or put out to nurse by the parish, died in still greater numbers. . . . The problem of deserted children—children exposed in the streets, orphans, and the children of poor parents—had long been an urgent one in London. . . . The Foundling Hospital [granted a charter in 1739] aimed at stopping the exposure, desertion, and murder of infants." The more morally abhorrent of these practices were clearly committed by mothers who were themselves desperately poor and abandoned by the infants' fathers. Few of Moll's moral protestations stand up to close examination, but child-murder and abandonment (along with committing incest and inducing abortion) seem genuinely shocking to her. Apparently, however, Moll's society did not see these acts as heinous crimes. In the eighteenth century it was not uncommon to see corpses of abandoned infants lying about on the streets, and in the rare instances that perpetrators were discovered and brought to court, they were usually let off with a light sentence. William Langer notes the implications of this phenomenon: "It seems reasonable in the light of this painful record to conclude that infanticide, covert or flagrant, was at least as important as celibacy in checking population growth from the middle of the 18th century to the middle of the 19th. *It is also evident that a marked change of attitude with respect to children, particularly the newborn, took place thereafter. What was then commonplace now seems intolerable cruelty.*"

An attitude of relative indifference to the fate of young children in this period extends even to parents of considerable wealth and sensibility. Numerous instances up through the seventeenth century attest to the continuity of the practice of sending children away from home at an early age to be nursed, schooled, or trained in another household. Although, like many other traditions, this one was beginning to disintegrate during the period in which Moll was raising her children, the child-centered home we are used to had clearly not replaced it. Children were often sent away from the best of motives: their mothers were ill and could not nurse them, they were sent to the country because cities were the centers of plague, or they were sent away for educational advantages. John Evelyn, for instance, was first sent to a neighbouring tenant's wife to be nursed for over a year "(in reguard for my Mother's weaknesse, *or rather custome of persons of quality*)," then "sent by my Father to Lewes in Sussex, to be with my Grandfather, with whom I pass'd my Childhood." Custom also decreed that even when children were raised at home, they were likely to be in the care of servants rather than their mothers. However affectionate or tenderhearted, mothers rarely absorbed themselves in personally raising their children. And when children died: "The carelessness of the nurses was often matched by an indifference on the part of parents, an attitude almost inevitably induced at a time when parents had so many children that they ceased to take an interest in them individually. 'Mrs. Thrale,' we are told, 'regarded the death of various daughters at school with great equanimity'; and Sir John Verney cheerfully remarked when two of his fifteen children died that he still had left a baker's dozen.

On such occasions as parents were not merely indifferent, they were often fatalistic, seeing in the death of their little ones the mysterious ways of God." Ignorance of obstetrical science and pediatrics as well as culpable neglect and cruelty created enormously high infant mortality rates. The probability that many children would not survive occasioned the indifference and fatalism of parents, but so too did a general psychological attitude. Children were not seen as having special and individual personalities, but as miniature adults, only duller and more burdensome.

It is in any case a gross distortion to list Moll's first five surviving children as "the two children discarded with her first husband's parents or the two children abandoned in Virginia or the boy left with her Bath gentleman." The first two verbs are loaded with meanings they cannot bear. There is a world of difference between saying (which is certainly true) that Moll does not wish to be personally responsible for her children and saying (what is not true) that she does not care what happens to them. To consign her children to the care of rich, doting, and settled grandparents can readily be seen as a sign of responsibility rather than irresponsibility; neither Moll's words nor her actions in these cases prove her to be morally culpable. Nor are they inconsistent with her words about "unnatural mothers," whom she defines as those who try to induce abortion or turn their children over to custodians without seeing that they will be well-tended rather than neglected or destroyed. Moreover, Moll speaks of the need of children for "an assisting hand, whether of the mother, *or some body else*" (my italics). Her phrasing is compatible with that of modern child psychologists, who speak of "mothers or mother-substitutes" and of "mother-figures" rather than exclusively of natural mothers. All the evidence provided by her own words, as well as those of her contemporaries and the scientists and historians of our own period, suggests that Moll is neither unnatural, culpable, nor unfeminine in her indifference to her children, certainly not by the standards of her own period, and probably not even by the standards of ours.

Investigation suggests that motherliness is not a purely innate trait, but a complex one, involving considerable admixtures of learning, experience, and accommodation to cultural expectations. Many normal women do not experience maternal feelings before their children are born; love for their offspring may not develop until after birth, during the nursing process, or even later in their interaction with their infants. Other scientists report that "many prospective parents take up the responsibilities of parenthood soberly, not necessarily with exhilaration," and note further that an eager desire to procreate may sometimes mask unhealthy and immature attitudes rather than express feminine maturity and tenderness.

It is clear that there is a wide range of appropriate, "normal," female responses to the role of motherhood, or, in technical phraseology, research indicates a "large number of intrapsychic, interpersonal, and cultural variables that converge in the enterprise of being a parent." For instance, in studies on the motherly traits of nonhuman primates—in whom one might expect to find maternal instinct in a purer form than in human mothers—it has been found that mothers who themselves have neither received mothering nor had an opportunity to observe or practice often prove to be totally inadequate mothers themselves, and are indifferent or abusive to their children. Investigation of the behavior of human mothers supports this finding. Moll is herself an example of a woman deprived of maternal care in infancy. Even without bringing this background information to bear, it seems clear that she does not forego her claim to femininity by bearing children mainly because her society expects her to while it provides her with no means of contraception and no other source of gratification.

Moll, however, sometimes exhibits considerable sentiment over parting with her children, thereby giving rise to charges of hypocrisy. She tells us that "it was death to me to part with the child" of her Bath lover, and that only "with a heavy heart and many a tear" did she relinquish the son of Jemy, her Lancashire husband, to the care of a nurse in the country. But these protestations together with her later pleasure in meeting her son in Virginia have causes other than hypocritical ones, not the least of which is that Moll, like many people, mellows as she ages. When she is young she wishes to be carefree, and, believing that she will give birth many times in the future, displays no interest in her children. The children over whom she waxes sentimental are, in contrast, born to her in her late thirties and forties, and are more precious to her partly because each may be her last. Moreover, the children of her later years are the offspring of men for whom she cared far more than she did her earlier husbands. These variables seem powerful reasons for considering her differing attitudes as humanly inconsistent but not as incredible or unforgivable. Even her attitude towards her son in Virginia, assuredly complicated though it is by her hearty interest in financial gain, need not be reduced wholly to economic interest. Given the predispositions of the period to romanticize gallant young men if not young children, it is surely understandable that Moll, seeing a "handsome comely young gentleman in flourishing circumstances," should be pleased with what "she hath wrought." To want to take pride in and make herself known to a prosperous independent adult is not inconsistent with seeing a dependent infant as an unpleasant burden she is pleased to leave behind her.

In fact all Moll's attitudes towards her children are readily comprehensible in terms of her sex, her age, and her culture: she is indifferent to them when both she and they are young, she is concerned about their welfare but uninterested in rearing them herself, and she responds to them when they are thriving or when they are the children of men whom she cares for. One would hardly want to claim that Moll is an exemplary mother; nonetheless, her attitudes and actions fall well within the range of normal, feminine behavior.

MOLL'S CHANGE OF LIFE

Moll's most protracted illness occurs at the end of her marriage career. Many readers find it and its startling conclusion—her entry into her criminal career—improbable and ill-motivated, but the text provides a number of clues to causes specifically related to her femininity. Moll describes her illness in a passage whose style recaptures the distraction she is recalling:

> But my case was indeed deplorable . . . I saw nothing before me but the utmost distress, and this represented it self so lively to my thoughts that it seem'd as if it was come before it was really very near. . . .
>
> In this distress I had no assistant, no friend to comfort or advise me, I sat and cried and tormented myself night and day; wringing my hands, and sometimes raving like a distracted woman; and indeed I have often wonder'd it had not affected my reason, for I had the vapours to such a degree that my understanding was sometimes quite lost in fancies and imagination.
>
> I liv'd two years in this dismal condition, wasting that little I had, weeping continually over my dismal circumstances, and as it were only bleeding to death.

This passage follows another highly revealing one:

> I foresaw the blow, and was extremely oppress'd in my mind, for I saw evidently that if he died I was undone.
>
> I had had two children by him and no more, for it began to be time for me to leave bearing children, for I was now eight and forty, and I suppose if he had liv'd I should have had no more.
>
> I was now left in a dismal and disconsolate case indeed, and in several things worse than ever. First, it was past the flourishing time with me when I might expect to be courted for a mistress; that agreeable part had declin'd some time, and the ruins only appear'd of what had been.

Taken together, these passages describe a constellation of female tribulations that makes Moll's anxiety perfectly comprehensible. At one and the same time she has lost her husband, her means of livelihood, her child-bearing capacity, her sexual attractiveness. The loss of any one of these would be a major blow; the loss of all of them together represents the loss of every source of security and gratification she is entitled to expect. Although these losses are tightly intertwined, it is worthwhile attempting to separate out and comment on each in order to emphasize the import and the specifically feminine qualities of this crisis.

Ian Watt professes difficulty in understanding Moll's conflicting feelings during her marriage to her fifth husband: "Moll's life with him is treated as a brief and wholly self-contained episode whose emotional premise does not have to be reconciled with other features of her life and character." Yet Moll's expressed satisfaction with this marriage and her grief upon the banker's death are surely not perplexing. The banker is "a quiet, sensible, sober man, virtuous, modest, sincere, and in his business diligent and just." He has, moreover, courted her with persistence, and has fallen in love with her (*her* and not her money) when she is forty-three years old "and did not look the better for my age, nor for my rambles to Virginia and back again" and when "nothing offered" for a long time despite her anxious attention to her prospects. Moll has found to her dismay that success in her matrimonial career has become increasingly more difficult to achieve as she ages. Unlike her earlier manner of proceeding—when time was on her side—her search for her last two husbands is attended by an air of desperation. Her Bath interlude makes her several hundred pounds richer, but six years older. Her desperation overcomes her normal caution and accounts for her falling victim to Jemy's ruse, but at least she has prudently kept the eager banker dangling lest her Lancashire adventure misfire. Given these circumstances, no wonder that despite her passion for Jemy, Moll responds eagerly to the banker's continuous opportunings and marries him with vast relief, thinking she is settled pleasurably and safely for life. And no wonder, then, that his death casts her into profound depression.

As we might expect, Moll dwells on her "dismal condition" primarily in financial terms. Yet the most convincing proof of the seriousness of her distress, marking it off from all the setbacks that have intervened since her first major illness, is what she does *not* say: she does *not* tally up her assets, a recurrent ritual here conspicuous by its absence. She alludes to this omission by confessing that her fears outstripped reality, that her actual capital exceeded her fancied perception of it, and that she only aggravated her financial condition by allowing her fears to paralyse her. But her exceptional misery *is* warranted: she ends this marriage with less capital than ever before and she has literally no prospect of maintaining or increasing it. She has come to the close of the only career society has allowed her.

Together with the loss of her financial dowry, Moll has lost her sexual endowments—her ability to bear children and her attractiveness. All her marketable assets have gone, and she naturally becomes extremely anxious about her future. However uninterested she is in her children as persons, her ability to create them has given her her main value in the eyes of society. The loss of this immensely significant role naturally causes an immense loss of self-esteem. The immediate strain she has suffered tending her husband in his decline has accelerated the natural process of aging, and she suffers not only a financial crisis, but a crisis of self-confidence. These biological processes affect many women in much the same way. For the underlying cause of Moll's depression is surely her inevitable involvement in the female condition: Moll is undergoing her climacterium.

There is considerable controversy in current psychosexual research concerning the extent to which climacteric depression is the result of physiological change or of cultural conditioning, and whether traditionally oriented women or women discontented with their feminine role are likely to suffer more severely. Whatever the balance of causes, there is general agreement that depression is unquestionably a normal fate of women during this stage in their aging process. According to Helene Deutsch, "almost every woman in the climacterium goes through a shorter or longer phase of depression." Although some men may also suffer middle-age depression, they do not as a group experience the loss of biosexual function and attractiveness and the loss of cultural value so absolutely nor respond to it so acutely as the generality of women.

The two writers of classic psychosexual studies of the climacterium, Helene Deutsch and Therese Benedek, agree upon two tendencies often accompanying responses to the climacterium that have special bearing upon Moll's experience. The first is that a woman's manner of reacting to her climacterium is likely to manifest itself as a more exaggerated version of a life-long pattern. That is, women who have earlier responded to their female role with depression or psychosomatic illness will respond to the onset of their climacterium in a similar but more intense form. Moll's two-year period of intense distress is therefore grounded in psychological probability. It is not mere fictional license or a lazy way of transporting her to the age of fifty. The second relevant point of agreement is that women respond to the end of their climacteric experience with a sense of relief and release that often takes the form of a drastic and even incongruous change in their life styles, interests, and behavior. This finding suggests an important reason for Moll's entry into her criminal career. Economic motives play a large role in spurring her on in this career, but as is evident from her own perplexity about why she continues to steal once her financial prosperity is assured, they do not wholly explain her behavior. Her criminal expertise provides her with intellectual and emotional satisfaction, a sense of achievement, and constant stimulation; she has found compensation for the loss of her roles as wife and mother, roles now denied to her by society and biology.

The particular details of Moll's criminal career are not especially relevant to the question of her femininity. On the other hand, none of her exploits or attitudes is inconsistent with her female role. She harbors no grudge against society, and accepts her difficulties without bitterness. Ian Watt is correct in saying that Moll rarely displays the characteristics of a criminal, for she sees herself not as an outcast but as a successful career woman, finding gratification in a new and challenging role. Her professionalism is thoroughgoing: she passes through a nervous apprenticeship period, then a period when she refines upon her teachers and learns to specialize, and finally becomes a "mastercraftsman." Her thieving career provides her with a truly absorbing activity and a reliable protector, as her earlier years had not. Moll's change of life commences with a shattering confluence of difficulties deeply rooted in the female condition, to which she, in common with many other women, responds first with paralysing depression, followed by relief, release, and the start of a new life.

THE BEST YEARS OF HER LIFE

Moll's criminal career comes to an abrupt close with her entry into Newgate prison. Her torpor in Newgate is readily understandable. She has arrived at the most absolute of the seeming impasses that had occasioned her earlier illnesses. On this occasion, her crisis has a religious context; it appears to represent the hardness of heart that precedes her confession, her experience of "secret surprising joy," and her spiritual repentance. Yet she describes her state "of the compleatest misery on earth" in terms very reminiscent of her earlier withdrawals into extreme passivity: "I degenerated into stone ... . a certain strange lethargy of soul possess'd me; I had no trouble, no apprehensions, no sorrow about me, the first surprise was gone. I was, I may well say, I know not how; my senses, my reason, nay, my conscience, were all asleep." This "strange lethargy of soul" must be seen as a significant part of a lifelong pattern.

This crisis is most interesting not for its symptoms but because of the manner of Moll's recovery. During the period when she is still unrepentant, a significant event rouses her from her lethargy—not a religious experience but the reappearance of Jemy, her highwayman-husband. Moll reiterates its effect four times: "In the middle of this harden'd part of my life, I had another sudden surprize, which call'd me back a little to that thing call'd sorrow, which, indeed, I began to be past the sense of before. . . . Nothing could express the amazement and surprize I was in, when the first man that came out I knew to be my Lancashire husband. . . . I was struck dumb at the sight. . . . The surprize of this thing only struck deeper in my thoughts, and gave me stronger reflections than all that had befallen me before." This experience revivifies Moll: "in a word, I was perfectly chang'd, and became another body." In comparison with *this* "secret, surprizing joy," Moll's subsequent description of her religious penitence is secondary and pallid.

Moll ascribes her rebirth to her sense of having been the occasion of Jemy's criminal career and capture: "This gentleman's misfortunes I plac'd all to my own account"; "I was overwhelm'd with grief for him; my own case gave me no disturbance compar'd to this, and I loaded myself with reproaches on his account." Moll's penitent love for Jemy is the foundation for her recovery. To notice this is to see the episode as an organic part of the narrative. Interpreted this way, it also makes the characterization of Moll at this point more convincing, and indeed more feminine. Receptivity to the softening effects of love is by no means exclusively a feminine trait. However, the details Moll provides serve to remind us of her capacity for love and tenderness, and they remind us too of the passionate attachments she has had to her first seducer, to her Bath gentleman, and especially to the younger Jemy. Coming to a crucial point in her life, this experience re-awakens latent tendencies which her struggle to conform to the role society demanded of her required that she suppress.

Moll's experience of renewal brings with it her capacity for practical action, and the subsequent scenes show her rallying Jemy from *his* lethargy, making arrangements for their comfortable passage to America, and providing the conditions for their successful experience as "new people in a new world." Her final American experience is the crowning happiness of her life. She has found an exciting, socially desirable, and rewarding outlet for her energies, talents, and feelings. Her earlier matrimonial career was uncertain and restrictive, her criminal career morally distressing and dangerous; neither fully satisfied her. Not at all unaware of Jemy's weaknesses, she displays tenderness, trust, and generosity towards him. She is indeed positively uxorious. In her old age, Moll reaches the culmination of her fortunes. If this is a sentimental conclusion, it is also one that is psychologically credible and satisfying, both in relation to her past experiences and to her consistently feminine behavior.

Moll's improbably crowded and sensational career has tended to obscure the ways in which her behavior, aspirations, and responses are consonant with and explicable by attention to the nature and limitations of the conventional female role. No woman typically runs through five husbands, several colorful careers, and a miscellany of adventures that includes living with gypsies, committing incest, bearing innumerable children, and suffering many financial disasters, and yet manages to live happily ever after and tell her tale with great aplomb. Strict conformity to matters of fact and to notions of genteel propriety would have required that any one of these sets of experiences consign Moll to bitterness, genteel poverty, ruin, or death—and the result would have been a tragic story, or more probably none at all. Hindsight should allow us to see that Defoe has romanticized the details of Moll's life and the degree to which good fortune attended it, but has sympathetically and convincingly rendered the underlying actualities of women's role. As Virginia Woolf writes, "Whatever his ideas upon the position of women, they are an incidental result of his chief virtue, which is that he deals with the important and lasting side of things and not with the passing and trivial." Moll's stubborn instinct for self-preservation manifests itself not in freedom from the requirements of the female role but in refusal to give way to the depressing consequences that too often surround it. She never willingly seeks adventures; all of them are thrust upon her by the necessities of her condition. Her ability to weather her crises with stamina, perseverance, and buoyancy is, in itself, a tribute to the very femininity—unglamorous but not inglorious—that modern readers deny her.

Openness and Complexity in *Moll Flanders*

Maximillian E. Novak

In *Lavengro,* George Borrow tells of his encounter with an old woman who kept a fruit stall on a London Bridge. He notices that she is reading a book "intently" and then finds himself grasped by her as he leans over the edge to see a boat caught in the swiftmoving waters. She has been watching him and concluded that he was a pickpocket down on his luck who decided to put an end to his life. He enters into conversation with her and discovers that she has a son at Botany Bay as a transported felon and that she sees no harm in stealing. In fact, she offers to act as a fence for any handkerchiefs he might have taken that day. Her views on theft are conditioned by her continued love for her thieving son who certainly would not do anything wrong and by her admiration for the heroine of the book she reads so eagerly—Moll Flanders. To the author's question about the "harm" in theft, she responds:

> "no harm in the world, dear! Do you think my own child would
> have been transported, if there had been any harm in it? and
> what's more, would the blessed woman in the book here have
> written her life as she has done, and given it to the world, if there
> had been any harm in faking? She, too, was what they call a thief
> and a cutpurse; ay, and was transported for it, like my dear son;
> and do you think she would have told the world so, if there had
> been any harm in the thing? Oh, it is a comfort to me that the
> blessed woman was transported, and came back—for come back

From *Realism, Myth, and History in Defoe's Fiction.* © 1983 by the University of Nebraska Press.

she did, and rich too—for it is an assurance to me that my dear son, who was transported too, will come back like her."

"What was her name?"

"Her name, blessed Mary Flanders."

Borrow, who has told his readers how he learned to read by his fascination with *Robinson Crusoe,* offers to buy the book from her as soon as he discovers in it "the air, the style, the spirit" of Defoe, but she refuses to sell it. "Without my book," she tells him, "I should mope and pine, and perhaps fling myself into the river." Instead, for six pence, she allows him to read it whenever he comes by. After some "wicked boys" try to steal the book from her, the old fruit seller loses some of her enthusiasm for the work, but the one time that Borrow, or his autobiographical hero, takes advantage of the chance to read, he finds himself so engrossed in it that hours pass by without his taking his eyes off the pages before him.

Now Borrow is engaging in some mythmaking of his own in creating the old fruit seller, who lives courageously on her slender earnings. Not surprisingly, it is the mythical Moll Flanders who is perceived by the old woman. She knows nothing about the warnings against stealing that Borrow points out to her. She reads it as a fairy tale, noticing only the "funny parts" and reaping from it a fund of hope that keeps her optimistic in spite of the grim facts of her life. Only when she begins to lose hope, which occurs after the attempted theft of the book, does she turn from it and agree to the author's offer to buy her a Bible in its place.

From some standpoints the old fruit woman is a bad reader, but what she perceives in *Moll Flanders* is certainly present in Defoe's work. This is the Moll who will not allow her difficulties to plunge her into despair, who rises above her situation to become a success—a successful servant, mistress, wife, thief, whore, plantation owner, and mother. Whatever warnings he wanted to give to thieves, he was more intent on telling them that they could find new lives in a New World. And Defoe knew that his audience tended to find a kind of subversive heroism in the new breed of thief and pirate that emerged at the start of the eighteenth century. Defoe excused many of Moll's acts on the grounds of poverty and necessity and, up to a point, gave the audience what they wanted.

I

Borrow does not tell us what edition of *Moll Flanders* it is that the old woman reads over and over again. If it was long enough to occupy Borrow for a number of hours, it was not one of the brief chapbook versions produced toward the end of the eighteenth century, but it may not have been Defoe's original work for all of that. Yet *Moll Flanders* received even briefer treatment in the ballad versions. The one that follows even deletes part of Defoe's title:

The Misfortunes of Moll Flanders

MOLL Flanders born in Newgate by man it is said.
Her tricks & fine manners I mean for to display
Seventeen times she was a lewd woman 5 times she was a
    wife,
And a slave to Virginia she was condemned for life.

For fam'd Shoplifting she surely bore the belle
For beauty & for artfulness none could her excell
To her own brother once was marry'd, dreadful tale to tell,
At Hounslow, and at Finchley, did often cut a swell.

The pitcher so often to the well it came home, broke at last.
Moll Flanders famous husband at length was try'd and cast,
The facts against him were so plain and awful did appear.
He at Tyburn suffer'd death for this crime as we hear.

A slave at Virginia she handled the Hoe,
Amongst West Indian Negroes she suffered many a blow,
An Eye witness to the cruelties that was inflicted there
She wish'd herself at home again upon her native shore.

But Providence that reigns above on her cast an eye,
Her mistress shewed her favour shed many a bitter sigh,
Though her misfortunes they were great she proved fortunate
    at last
Lived honest and dy'd penitent lament her follies past.

Such an extraordinary character you never heard before.
And so you will say I know full well when this book you do
    read o'er,
No one would scarcely credit what she did undergo.
Be warn'd by her you young and gay & honestly pursue.

Defoe obviously had nothing to do with this piece of doggerel, but it is useful to see what remains of his novel. She is still the child born in New-gate, still the great beauty as well as the great sinner, and still the success in the end. But except for her sex and the incestuous marriage to her brother, most of the events fit the life of Colonel Jack better than they do Moll's. Defoe's Moll is different. Moll's husband is not hanged, she never handles a hoe or has to labor in America, and she is not rescued from life among the slaves by her "mistress." One might well wonder if this was the ballad that inspired Hogarth's Idle Apprentice to commit his crimes.

Defoe's *Moll Flanders* has a brief but open ending in which she tells of her return to England and the penitence for her wicked life that the preface puts in doubt. Like most of the abridgments and chapbook versions, the ballad tries to give it more of an ending with a report of her death and a moral on her life. Borrow's old fruit seller focuses on Moll's return to England at the end as an indication that her son will return from Australia to live rich and happy in England, though most of the abridgments, if they do not have her die after a long and happy life in Virginia, bring her back to her husband's lands in Ireland where she is supposed to die after her husband and be buried in the same grave with him. The longest of the abridgments, *The History of Laetitia Atkins,* published in 1776 and ascribed to Defoe on the title page actually prints her will with its generous gifts to the servants and its assignment of most of her property to her husband's brother, William Carrol, along with an account of her pious death surrounded by "eminent divines."

All of this suggests that *Moll Flanders* has a mythic life of its own. Like Betteredge, who consults *Robinson Crusoe* as a holy book that will provide him with all the answers to the problems of life, Borrow's fruit woman treats her copy of *Moll Flanders* as a magical text. If Moll Flanders could steal, there could be nothing wrong with theft. When Borrow brings the old woman a Bible to replace *Moll Flanders* as the book by which the woman will guide her life, he replaces one magical text with another. The Bible, however, begins to function for her only after she recalls a dim commandment from her youth: "Thou shalt not steal." Only after she begins to worry about her life and values does she begin to tire of the subversive text by which she has been living.

Of course, Borrow's insistence that she had been misreading Defoe's work has its point too. She transforms Moll into a patron saint of criminals—"blessed Mary Flanders." She sees humor in it, but she is incapable of following the subtleties of Defoe's language, and she simply ignores Moll's direct moralizing on crime. In her own way, she edits as she reads and transforms Defoe's novel into her private rendition of the short, chapbook versions that provided little more than the myth of the clever and successful criminal. That is hardly what *Moll Flanders* is really about. I want to turn now to examine what an ideal reader might discover beyond the myth.

II

> *Behold the cruel Hand of death,*
> *Hath snatch'd away* Elizabeth.
> *Twelve Years she was an arant Whore;*
> *Was sometimes rich, and sometimes poor;*
> *Which made her, when she'd no Relief,*
> *Be full as many Years a Thief.*
> *In this Carier of Wickedness,*
> *Poor* Betty *always had success;*
>> From a chapbook version
>> of *Moll Flanders*

I leave the Readers of these things to their own just Reflections, which they will be more able to make effectual than I, who so soon forgot my self, and am therefore but a very indifferent Monitor.

DEFOE, Moll Flanders

Among the many contemporary attacks on Daniel Defoe, one of more than usual interest, entitled *The Republican Bullies* (1705), pretended to report a dialogue between Defoe (Mr. Review) and John Tutchin, author of a journal called *The Observator*. After stating that he wants no part of sword fights, Defoe explains that he is more adept at destroying his enemies with irony:

REV. No man would dispute the Prize with you, if downright
Billingsgate was the Weapon to gain by it. He's the
Champion for a Modern Readers Mony, that can cut a
Throat with a Feather, that can wound the sacred Order
by way of Expostulations and fling Dirt upon them by
Dint of Irony as I have done.

OBS. The only Figure in Rhetorick that you are Master of!
More thanks to Nature than Art, who has given it to
you, without so much as letting you know that it is One.

That his contemporaries recognized that his "peculiar Talent" lay in presenting effective arguments through the use of irony, satire, and fiction is obvious enough to anyone who has studied the numerous, grudging compliments given him by his enemies. His reputation as a poet and a pamphleteer declined only when his work for the government forced him into such dull repetition and absurd contradiction that even his amazing wit and intelligence had to fail him.

But whatever his contemporaries may have thought of him, two facts have become apparent from the recent critical debates over *Moll Flanders:* (1) that he may have been ironic in some of his pamphlets is no guarantee that he was being ironic in *Moll Flanders;* (2) that his contemporaries regarded his manner as ironic does not mean that what he did satisfied some modern critics' concepts of irony. Until some universally acceptable definition of irony can be established, critics will continue to disagree, and I have no intention in this chapter to revive a discussion that has proved so inconclusive. Instead, I want to examine in detail some of the complexities of language and narrative in *Moll Flanders* that have led me and some other critics to doubt that they are dealing with a fiction involving a straightforward fictional confession and imagine that Moll's was the kind of ironic narrative Defoe might have inherited from picaresque fiction directly or through the influence of the picaresque on criminal biography.

Some useful information about the genesis of Defoe's novel was provided in 1968 by Gerald Howson, whose article in *TLS,* "Who Was Moll Flanders?" tells us a great deal about the criminals who formed the basis for Defoe's narrator. Moll Flanders, we learn, was imaginatively constructed from several women criminals of the time, particularly two known by the names Moll King and Callico Sarah. Since Defoe was visiting his friend, the publisher Mist, in Newgate at the same time these two ladies were there, he would have had numerous opportunities to converse with them. Moll King managed to survive from five to eight sentences of transportation without being hanged, and if some critics have discovered in Moll Flanders's life a mythic, symbolic sense of human endurance, they might well feel justified.

Defoe may even have taken his heroine's name from an indirect combination of the names of these two women, since *Flanders* was the name for a Flemish lace, a contraband article figuring in one of Moll Flanders's thefts. Howson allows that the contemporary advertisement for *The History of Flanders with Moll's Map,* a reference to the work of the cartographer Herman Moll, may have given Defoe his initial idea, but he advances his suggestion concerning the relation between calico and lace as being more relevant, and I agree. Now the genesis of Defoe's title may seem completely unimportant, but I want to argue that this suggestive use of language is one of the most important elements in *Moll Flanders* and a key to its complexity.

Though Defoe's lapses from consistency have often caused his artistic integrity to be called into question, he was a writer deeply concerned with language and the meaning of words—the way an understanding of subtle shifts in meaning distinguishes the good writer from the bad. Let us suppose for the moment that Defoe set out to present a character who passes over certain points of her life with evasive remarks and comes close to lying about others. How would it be possible to handle the language of narrative in such a way that something resembling a true view of the events would be apparent to the reader? Wayne Booth has pointed out the difficulties with proving ironic intent in a novel written in the first person, and Defoe was not above solving this problem in pamphlets employing a persona by ending them with a direct confession of what he called "Irony." But realistic fiction would prevent a device of this kind. What Defoe needed was a method of making meaning transparent without sacrificing the integrity of his point of view.

One way out was through a complex use of language and what Defoe called "Inuendo," by which he meant all indirect methods of communication from irony to meiosis. If we turn to the point in Defoe's novel when Moll has been abandoned by the lover she picked up at Bath, some of the complications involved will be clear. After receiving a note from him cutting off the affair, Moll writes a letter telling him that she would never be able to recover from the blow of parting from him, that she not only approved of his repentance but wished "to Repent as sincerely as he had done." All she needs is fifty pounds to return to Virginia. Moll confesses at once that what she said "was indeed all a Cheat," and that "the business was to get this last Fifty Pounds of him," but she does moralize on the situation:

> And here I cannot but reflect upon the unhappy Consequence of too great Freedoms between Persons started as we were, upon the pretence of innocent intentions, Love of Friendship, *and the like;* for the Flesh has generally so great a share in those Friendships, that it is great odds but inclination prevails at last over the most solemn Resolutions and that Vice breaks in at the breaches of Decency, which really innocent Friendship ought to preserve with the greatest strictness; but I leave the Readers of these things to their own just Reflections, which they will be more able to make effectual than I, who so soon forgot my self, and am therefore but a very indifferent Monitor.

Moll's willingness to confess that any admonitions coming from her about manners and morals might well be regarded sceptically should put the reader on guard at once. Would we want to hear morality preached by Moll King or Callico Sarah? And after all, Moll has just testified to her dishonesty. Surely at this point simple solutions (e.g., it is Defoe with his somewhat questionable puritan moral standards speaking) will not work.

There are also disturbing stylistic elements in the passage that might prevent the reader from regarding it as a straightforward confession. Take the phrase, "Love of Friendship, *and the like.*" One might also think that Moll was being witty, that "*and the like*" was intended to imply by ironic understatement all the possible kinds of discourses leading ultimately to seduction. Although Professor Watt has warned us against reading into Defoe what is not there, this is an important element in Moll's narrative. She is always qualifying words in order to clarify the distinction between the apparent meaning of a word and the reality behind it. The brother she lived with in incest is "my Brother, *as I now call him,*" the first woman who takes care of her is "my Mistress Nurse, *as I call'd her,*" the trunk she steals from a Dutchman is "my Trunk, *as I call'd it.*" Whether or not Defoe actually added the italics to these phrases (as he did occasionally in the one extensive manuscript of his that we have), they were obviously intended to suggest the disparity between what something is called and what it is, and to call attention to the narrator's own awareness of this.

Similar to these kinds of phrases is her simple remark, "I WAV'D the Discourse" when her Bank Manager sums up the character of his wife with the remark, "she that will be *a Whore* will be *a Whore,*" or her summation of her reaction to the entire tale of this sad cuckold, "Well, I pitied him, and wish'd him well rid of her, and still would have talk'd of my Business." The tone of impatience (the Bank Manager is married and therefore unavailable at this point) is clear enough. Defoe *is* conveying a great deal, then, through tone and language.

In fact Moll is extraordinarily playful in her use of language. When she tries to avoid joining a gang of counterfeiters, she remarks, "tho' I had declin'd it with the greatest assurances of Secresy in the World, they would have gone near to have murther'd me, to make sure Work, and make themselves easy, *as they call it;* what kind of easiness that is, they may best Judge that understand how easy Men are, that can murther People to prevent Danger." And the section in which she enters the home for unwed mothers is full of such implications. After the Governess has assured her that she need not worry about the care of her child if she puts it out to a nurse recommended by the house and that she must behave as "other conscientious Mothers," Moll, who is careful to separate herself from "all those Women who consent to the disposing their Children out of the way, *as it is call'd,*" comments on her Governess's language: "I understood what she meant by conscientious Mothers, she would have said conscientious Whores; but she was not willing to disoblige me." Moll tells herself that, at least technically, she was married, but then merely contents herself with distinguishing herself from other prostitutes ("the Profession") by her still tender heart. Even the affectionate use of the term *Mother* for her Governess is suspect. Though she might have a right to that title by her affectionate treatment of Moll, or by being Moll's "Mother Midnight," that is, her midwife, the name was usually given to the madam of a brothel. In fact their dialogues resemble nothing so much as those between Mother Cress-well and Dorothea, bawd and neophyte, in *The Whore's Rhetorick* (1683). They, too, refer to each other as mother and daughter, and Moll's Mother-Governess is not above being a bawd as well as an abortionist and a fence.

Perhaps the way in which Moll describes the suggestion of an abortion and her rejection of it gives the best clues to the complex use of language in Defoe's novel:

> The only thing I found in all her Conversation on these Subjects, that gave me any distaste, was, that one time in Discoursing about my being so far gone with Child, and the time I expected to come, she said something that look'd as if she could help me off with my Burthen sooner, if I was willing; or in *English,* that she could give me something to make me Miscarry, if I had a desire to put an end to my Troubles that way; but I soon let her see that I abhorr'd the Thoughts of it; and to do her Justice, she put it off so cleverly, that I could not say she really intended it, or whether she only mentioned the practice as a horrible thing; for she couch'd her words so well, and took my meaning so quickly, that she gave her Negative before I could explain my-self.

Moll used the same pun a few pages before; if the reader failed to catch it the first time, he might be at least as clever as Moll's Governess and pick it up the second time around. One can assume, then, that, at times, Moll converses in double-entendres and expects her listeners and readers to understand them.

Such word play is not uncommon in Defoe's narrative. As I have indicated elsewhere, Moll points to her misunderstanding of the use of the word *Miss* by the wife of the mayor who comes to visit her when she is a child in Colchester: "The Word Miss was a Language that had hardly been heard of in our School, and I wondered what sad Name it was she call'd me." It is a sad word because it says something about her future quest after gentility and her future life as a prostitute. In much the same way, thinking of the friend who has passed her off as a woman of fortune, Moll tells of how she decides to take a trip to Bath. "I took the Diversion of going to the *Bath,*" she remarks, "for as I was still far from being old, so my Humour, which was always Gay, continu'd so to an Extream; and being now, *as it were,* a Woman of Fortune, tho' I was a Woman without a Fortune, I expected something, or other might happen in my way, that might mend my Circumstances, as had been my Case before." Another instance of this type of word play comes in the section on the counterfeiters. Speaking of her refusal to join the gang, Moll remarks that

> the part they would have had me have embark'd in, was the most dangerous Part; I mean that of the very working the Dye, as they call it, which had I been taken, had been certain Death, and that at a Stake, *I say,* to be burnt to Death at a Stake; so that tho' I was to Appearance, but a Beggar; and they promis'd Mountains of Gold and Silver to me, to engage; yet it would not do; it is True, if I had been really a Beggar, or had been desperate as when I began, I might perhaps have clos'd with it, for what care they to Die, that can't tell how to Live?

The phrase, "working the Dye," which James Sutherland calls a "grim pun" in his edition of *Moll Flanders,* meant to stamp the coin. A terrible death awaits those who would gamble or stake their lives on such an occupation, and in the midst of her punning, Moll is careful to remark that "they" use the term "working the Dye," not she. This is her way of separating herself from such awful people.

It is passages like these that lead the reader to suspect other double meanings. When Moll is made pregnant by her Bath Lover, he assumes the name of Sir Walter Cleave, and Moll says that she was made as comfortable as she would have been had she "really been my Lady *Cleave.*" In addition to whatever sexual significance might be attached to this word by a wary reader, a "cleave" is defined as "a forward or wanton woman" in Francis Grose's *A Classical Dictionary of the Vulgar Tongue.* And significantly enough, in the rather pious chapbook versions of Moll Flanders, the name was changed to Clare.

At other times the issue is doubtful. Is Moll aware of any sexual significance in a phrase like that already quoted in Moll's reflections on her Bath Lover, that "Vice breaks in at the breaches of Decency?" If we regard Moll as being, at least in part, a comic figure, we would have to say that Defoe makes her use this phrase with some ambiguity. Is she supposed to understand certain implications in such language? Did Defoe? Having no definite solution, I will follow Moll and waive the discourse. But of Defoe's use of puns and word play as a method to convey subtle meanings playing underneath Moll's narrative there cannot be the slightest doubt.

III

If some passages raised doubts in the reader's mind, there is good reason for it: Moll, herself, is often undecided or uncertain about the way she should interpret the events of her life, and her language often reflects these doubts. She begins the story of her Bath lover's control over his sexual desires with a remark that reveals her undecided state. He has spent the night in bed with her entirely naked and without offering any advances that might be regarded as completely sexual in nature. Moll comments, "I OWN it was a noble Principle, but as it was what I never understood before, so it was to me perfectly amazing." Even if one understands by "noble Principle" something that cannot work in practice, we cannot come to such a decision until Moll's final condemnation of the entire relationship several pages later.

Such passages are complex not so much because of the language alone but because Defoe asks us to suspend our judgment on the meaning of certain words and phrases until the events themselves or Moll's last commentary clarifies the situation. Many of Moll's comments on her Governess are rich in this kind of momentary ambiguity. When the woman chosen by the Governess to tutor Moll in the art of thievery has been taken and sentenced to death, the emotions of the Governess have to be ambiguous, since the tutoress has enough information to save her own life by impeaching the Governess. Moll King saved her life several times in this manner. Moll Flanders does not render such a mixture of regret for the loss of a friend and apprehension for personal safety in anything resembling straight description:

> It is true, that when she was gone, and had not open'd her Mouth to tell what she knew; my Governess was easy as to that Point, and perhaps glad she was hang'd; for it was in her power to have obtain'd a Pardon at the Expence of her Friends; But on the other Hand, the loss of her, and the Sense of her Kindness in not making her Market of what she knew, mov'd my Governess to Mourn very sincerely for her: I comforted her as well as I cou'd, and she in return harden'd me to Merit more compleatly the same Fate.

Moll's bitterness is apparent enough, but the language is sometimes pointed, sometimes neutral in a situation that is inherently ambiguous. The Governess, whose life has been spared at this point and later threatened in the same way by Moll's capture, is sincere in her sorrow, but she does not undergo any change of heart. And Moll may be speaking of one point in the past, but she has her mind set on another point—her future sufferings in Newgate.

I will speak more fully of the problems of time in Moll's narrative later in this chapter, but it should be noted here that in passages such as these, Moll's narrative may be viewed ironically (by anyone's definition) on the present level of the told narrative, while functioning realistically as a record of the action as it is occurring. Many of the contradictions that appear in the novel are caused by the simple fact that even criminals and fences have to have a morality to live by. Polls among jail inmates revealing strong moral disapproval of crime are commonplace. As we shall see, such moral judgments need not indicate a permanent change of heart.

When Moll commits her "second Sally into the World," she tells of her experience in a manner that is even more demanding of complex understanding. Having led the little girl out of her way, Moll is confronted by the child's protests. She quiets these objections with the sinister remark, "I'll show you the way home." This piece of direct dialogue is given in a narrative scene to underscore its ironic implication—the possibility that to quiet the child while she was stealing the necklace she might have to murder her. After describing her horror at the impulse to murder, Moll tells of her psychological state after this robbery. "The last Affair," she says, "left no great Concern upon me," explaining that after all she did not harm the child and may have helped improve the care that the parents of the child would show in the future. And after estimating the value of the string of beads, Moll begins to extrapolate about the entire incident. The girl was wearing the necklace because the mother was proud; the child was being neglected by the mother, who had put her in the care of a maid; the maid was doubtless negligent and meeting her lover. And while all these palliations for her crime are being offered—and they sound peculiarly like crimes Moll might have been guilty of at other stages of her career—the "pretty little Child" has gradually become the "poor Child," "poor Lamb," and "poor Baby." In blaming everyone else but herself, Moll is revealing that her psychological involvement is far greater than she is willing to admit, and the energy that she exerts to deny her involvement is undercut verbally by the increasing sympathy she tries to arouse for the child.

As for blaming such moralizing on Defoe's simplemindedness, it should be pointed out that a later incident shows a similar unwillingness to accept guilt mingled with a more obvious callousness toward crime. When Moll seduces a Gentleman in a coach, she moralizes on the possibility that the man might have been seduced by a diseased prostitute. Her moralizing, it should be noted, is a blend of past and present reactions:

As for me, my Business was his Money, and what I could make of him, and after that if I could have found out any way to have done it, I would have sent him safe home to his House, and to his Family, for 'twas ten to one but he had an honest virtuous Wife, and innocent Children, that were anxious for his Safety, and would have been glad to have gotten him Home, and have taken care of him, till he was restor'd to himself; and then with what Shame and Regret would he look back upon himself? how would he reproach himself with associating himself with a Whore? pick'd up in the worst of all Holes, the Cloister, among the Dirt and Filth of the Town? how would he be trembling for fear he had got the Pox, for fear a Dart had struck through his Liver, and hate himself every time he look'd back upon the Madness and Brutality of his Debauch? how would he, if he had any Principles of Honour, as I verily believe he had, I say how would he abhor the Thought of giving any ill Distemper, if he had it, as for ought he knew he might, to his Modest and Virtuous Wife, and thereby sowing the Contagion in the Life-Blood of his Posterity?

What is curious about this is that Moll is substantially creating a fiction as she goes along in much the same manner as she did with the child she robbed. The fiction about the gentleman led astray by the prostitute is highly moral and has little or none of the word play that, as I have shown, is a customary part of Moll's narrative manner. But it is a fiction for all that, a story woven to cheer herself up in the past and present, and the more graphic it is, the more real it is for her.

And then Moll does something that we ought to expect. She betrays herself by telling a somewhat off-color story of how, by replacing his purse with one filled with tokens during sexual intercourse, a prostitute once managed to pick the pocket of a customer, even though he was on his guard. Doubtless she tells the sad story of the gentleman who might have picked up a diseased prostitute to her Governess in as moving terms as she tells it to the reader, for she described how that good lady "was hardly able to forbear Tears, to think how such a Gentleman run a daily Risque of being undone, every Time a Glass of Wine got into his Head." But the Governess is entirely pleased by the booty Moll has brought her from the gentleman, and after assuring Moll that the incident might "do more to reform him, than all the Sermons that ever he will hear in his life," she proceeds to arrange a liaison between Moll and the gentleman. It is impossible to think that Defoe was napping here. Moll and her Governess possess a great deal of morality, but they are criminals nevertheless, and Defoe never lets us forget it. Moll remains throughout the novel an "indifferent Monitor."

IV

During this discussion of the complexities of language and style in *Moll Flanders*, I have touched on the intricate temporal relationships in individual passages; now I want to turn to the larger issue of time in Defoe's narrative as a further example of Defoe's considerable skill. Most modern discussions of narrative technique in *Moll Flanders* begin with a version of the concept of the "double focus" suggested by Mendilow in his *Time and the Novel*. Mendilow suggested that both *Moll Flanders* and *Roxana* belonged to that type of novel in which, because the narrator is speaking of her youth, "one often senses the gap between the action and its record." Mendilow then remarked that "two characters are superimposed one upon the other, and the impression of the one who acts is coloured and distorted by the interpretations of the one who narrates," and that the "diaries" of Moll and Roxana as they would have been written in their youth would have been far different from these retrospective narratives. Some critics have disagreed with Mendilow's conclusions, but that is probably because they failed to remark that he adds later on that novels often "contain different degrees of pastness."

Certainly *Moll Flanders* is extraordinarily varied in treating levels of time, and a good example of the way we experience Moll's movement between such levels may be seen in the passages preceding the death of her Bank Manager husband. The basic technique is that of summary, but as she carries us breathlessly through the five years of happiness she had with him, she also supplies us with a vivid picture of her psychological state:

> I liv'd with this Husband in the utmost Tranquility; he was a Quiet, Sensible, Sober Man, Virtuous, Modest, Sincere, and in his Business Diligent and Just: His Business was in a narrow Compass, and his Income sufficient to a plentiful way of Living in the ordinary way; I do not say to keep an Equipage, and make a Figure as the World calls it, nor did I expect it, or desire it; for as I abhorr'd the Levity and Extravagance of my former Life, so I chose now to live retir'd, frugal, and within our selves; I kept no Company, made no Visits; minded my Family, and oblig'd my Husband; and this kind of Life became a Pleasure to me.

Such a passage is intended to show Moll's temporary conversion to the ideals of a middle-class marriage. But it also dips vividly into past experience. Unlike Moll's first lover, who carried her off in the coach of Sir W—— H——, her Gentleman Tradesman husband, who insisted in travelling in a "*Coach and Six,*" and her Lancashire Husband, Jemmy, who calls for her with his "Chariot . . . , with two Footmen in a good Livery," this husband offers her only the kind of comfort that she had always rejected. In this marriage she has rejected the "World" of fashion, which had been her envy from childhood, to find pleasure in what was Defoe's ideal—the private life of a contented family.

Defoe had stated such an ideal before, but nowhere so thoroughly as in his *Condoling Letter to the Tatler* (1710), in which he portrayed human happiness as a means illustrated by a thermometer of the human condition:

Madness,

Poverty,

Extravagence,

Excess or Profusion,

Waste,

Generous Liberality,

Plenty

FAMILY

Frugality,

Parsimony,

Niggardliness,

Covetousness,

Sordidly Covetous,

Wretchedness or Rich Poverty

Madness

> Here is the Word FAMILY in the Centre, which signifies the man, let his Circumstances be what it will, for every Man is a Family to himself. He is plac'd between *Plenty* and *Frugality*; a Blessed, Happy Medium, which makes Men beloved of all, respectd of the Rich, blessed by the Poor, useful to themselves, to their Country, and to their Posterity.

In Defoe's thermometer of well-being, madness through wealth or poverty stands at both the bottom and the top. Moll has truly achieved a state that she comes to recognize as ideal, even if it is not what she would want if she had her choice. She is soon close to a state of desperate poverty.

Those who have seen this as the psychological and structural middle of the novel can find justification both in Moll's moral career from this point on and in the narrative. For after this summary of her present condition, which is in itself so full of echoes of the past, Moll tells of her husband's bankruptcy in terms that move forward from the way the event "turn'd . . . [her] out into the World in a Condition the reverse of all that had been before it," goes back in time to narrate the cause of his troubles, and tells the reader the advice she gave him. One paragraph tells of his death in a manner that skillfully reverses the event and her forebodings: "It was in vain to speak comfortably to him, the Wound had sunk too deep, it was a Stab that touch'd the Vitals, he grew Melancholy and from thence Lethargick, and died; I foresaw the Blow, and was extremely oppress'd in my Mind, for I saw evidently that if he died I was undone." One of the remarkable things about Defoe's style in such passages is the way he can be both concise and repetitious at the same time, a technique that Lévi-Strauss has found to be the essential narrative quality of myth. Thus, when she recognizes her Lancashire Husband riding into the Inn where she is staying with her new husband, the Bank Manager, she says, "I knew his Cloaths, I knew his Horse, and I knew his Face." Nothing could be more dramatic and, without dwelling on her psychological state, tell us how she feels by what appears to be an external description. A similar process is at work in her account of the death of the Bank Manager. Moll is not merely telling the reader about the progress of his disease, she is explaining how she watched his decline with terror.

Much of this may be viewed as a question of style, but the important point is that Defoe was continually manipulating style to achieve narrative effects. He even changes tenses or makes use of contemporary grammatical forms that could stand for either present or past to attain a sense of immediacy in scenes of action. When a fire breaks out in the neighborhood of her Governess, Moll rushes to the scene to pick up what booty she can find:

> Away I went, and coming to the House I found them all in Confusion, you may be sure; I run in, and finding one of the Maids, Lord! Sweetheart, *said I,* how came this dismal Accident? Where is your Mistress? And how does she do? Is she safe? And where are the Children? I come from Madam—— to help you; away runs the Maid, Madam, madam, *says she,* screaming as loud as she cou'd yell, *here is a Gentlewoman come from Madam—— to help us:* The poor Woman half out of her Wits, with a Bundle under her Arm, and two little Children, comes towards me, *Lord Madam,* says I, let me carry the poor Children to Madam——, she desires you to send them; she'll take care of the poor Lambs, and immediately I takes one of them out of her Hand, and she lifts the other up into my arms; *ay, do for God*

sake, says she . . . and away she runs from out of her Wits, and the Maids after her, and away comes I with the two Children and the Bundle.

Some curiosities in Defoe's grammar have led older critics to comment on his homely style, but here Defoe is taking advantage either of what would be Moll's ungrammatical manner or simply sacrificing grammar to achieve a sense of hurry and excitement. Both seem to be present in the "away she runs . . . and away comes I" section so typical of Moll in her lighter moments.

In such a passage, of course, the use of dialogue is equally important for giving the feeling of action recreated in the present. If Defoe did not succeed in getting the kind of immediacy achieved by Richardson's technique of "writing to the present," he nevertheless attempted various methods of attaining a similar effect when he needed it. *Moll Flanders* differs from Defoe's two historical novels, *Memoirs of a Cavalier* and *A Journal of the Plague Year.* As I have attempted to show, both of these function in a specific historical time, although that time is made so dramatically cogent for the present as to make it serve a purpose similar to that of fulfilled vision or prophecy. And *Moll Flanders* is also different from *Roxana,* which, as we shall see, completely distorts historical time. Yet the seeming error in having Roxana's career function in both the era of the Restoration and the eighteenth century is certainly understandable, for Defoe wanted to contrast the dissolute court of Charles II with the luxury of his own time. If his transition from one period to the other would have to be achieved by a process that is opposed to any concept of realistic chronology, it was, nevertheless, an experiment that might have been worth trying.

Mendilow's formula, then, is good as far as it goes, but Defoe's world is always synchronic rather than diachronic. The past is imported into the present as a psychologically recreatable state. Hence Moll's reactions are indeed confused and ambiguous. Crusoe does not have the same difficulty separating his past from his present, and Roxana may vary between irony and passion in commenting on her past, but she is seldom without some kind of commentary. Moll's reaction to her past is somewhat reminiscent of the first person narrative of a shaman among the Kwakiutls that Franz Boas recorded. The Narrator, QāsElīd, begins as a skeptic. "Then it occurred to me," he states, "that I was the principal one who does not believe in all the ways of the shamans, for I had said so aloud to them. Now I had an opportunity by what they said that I should really learn whether they were real or whether they only pretended to be shamans." Eventually, after becoming a shaman himself, he finds that the cures he works are superior to those of other shamans and comes to believe that somehow he does have curative powers. The narrative reveals a development, yet were he to begin again, he would unquestionably start with his initial scepticism and the lying and fakery among shamans. Like QāsElīd, Moll responds dynamically and ambiguously to her own narrative, reliving her past life for the reader as she recreates it for herself in the present.

This is why her conversion to Christianity, which most students find questionable, is without much of the wit and complexity to be found in most sections of the novel. If we find that her life after conversion is not what we would expect of a good Christian, we share a feeling that the "editor" informs us may have considerable basis in fact. Perhaps Moll's concern and the reader's are too strong at these moments to allow for a definition of *Moll Flanders* as an ironic novel. Certainly it does not deserve such a name if that genre is to be limited to works like Fielding's *Jonathan Wild* or Ford's *The Good Soldier*. But Defoe has Moll relive her life, responding to the emotions of the moment as they reflect her previous emotions and experiences. And if she can be both the ideal convert and the wayward servant-whore-thief at the same time, she shares with the Kwakiutl shaman the natural ability to exist in a number of states simultaneously.

My comparison of QāsElīd and Moll might lead one to the conclusion that the actual thrust of Defoe's fiction was toward a simple mirroring of reality and real personality, though, as I have tried to demonstrate throughout, fictional reality is never simple. In fact, such an argument has been advanced by Ralph Rader, who discusses Moll and her narrative as a story of the "pseudo-factual type," one in which Defoe, as author, has disappeared to the extent that any judgment about the moral meaning of the work must remain ambiguous, because we accept Moll as a real person and her narrative as the product of her own pen. Since great fiction, by Rader's definition, must announce itself as artifact, *Moll Flanders* is the last of a tradition of "true stories" rather than the forerunner of the novel.

Such a view represents a misunderstanding of Defoe's art as well as of the tradition of literary history which, until the last half of the nineteenth century, always accorded picaresque fiction a secure, if low, position. It also constitutes a misunderstanding of the nature of Defoe's realism. His fictional rhetoric in *Moll Flanders* includes a central character who assumes not merely the particularity of an individual character but also the generality that makes for the prototype of the eternal female. Her endurance in chapbook form, her echo in James Joyce's Molly Bloom and Joyce Cary's Sara Monday of *Herself Surprised* is evidence of this. Moll's language conveys its meanings to the reader through the complexity of word play, innuendo, and ironic asides. And her contradictions, her presentation of various moral views of her actions in a manner that G. S. Starr has properly called "casuistry," provides a clearer view of the ethical significance of her actions and the ways they are to be judged by the reader than may be found in all but the most didactic novels.

V

I want to conclude this chapter by examining a passage that draws together some of the main ideas I have been discussing. Moll, whose tendency to work alone and whose cautious approach to her "Trade" has enabled her to survive and prosper as the greatest "Artist" of her time, tells how she almost went into a partnership that would have proven disastrous:

> I began to think that I must give over the Trade in Earnest; but my Governess, who was not willing to lose me, and expected great Things of me, brought me one Day into Company with a young Woman and a Fellow that went for her Husband, tho' as it appear'd afterwards she was not his Wife, but they were Partners it seems in the Trade they carried on; and Partners in something else too. *In short,* they robb'd together, lay together, were taken together, and at last were hang'd together.
>
> I Came into a kind of League with these two, by the help of my Governess, and they carried me out into three or four Adventures, where I rather saw them commit some Coarse and unhandy Robberies, in which nothing but a great Stock of impudence on their Side, and gross Negligence on the Peoples Side who were robb'd, could have made them Successful; so I resolv'd from that time forward to be very Cautious how I Adventur'd upon any thing with them; and indeed when two or three unlucky Projects were propos'd by them, I declin'd the offer, and perswaded them against it: One time they particularly propos'd Robbing a Watchmaker of 3 Gold Watches, which they had Ey'd in the Day time, and found the Place where he laid them; one of them had so many Keys of all kinds, that he made no Question to open the Place, where the Watchmaker had laid them; and so we made a kind of an Appointment; but when I came to look narrowly into the Thing, I found they propos'd breaking open the house; and this as a thing out of my Way, I

would not Embark in; so they went without me: They did get into the House by main Force, and broke up the lock'd Place where the Watches were, but found but one of the Gold Watches, and a Silver one, which they took, and got out of the House again very clear, but the Family being alarm'd cried out Thieves, and the Man was pursued and taken, the young Woman had got off too, but unhappily was stop'd at a Distance, and the Watches found upon her; and thus I had a second Escape, for they were convicted, and both hang'd, being old Offenders, tho' but young People; as *I said before,* that they robbed together, and lay together, so now they hang'd together, and there ended my new Partnership.

Such a passage would have amused Borrow's old fruit seller. She would have observed the mythic Moll Flanders in the clever thief who is contemptuous of her potential partners' incompetence as well as of the "gross Negligence on the Peoples Side who were robbed." Moll, who usually makes a distinction between herself and those whom she regards as common thieves, demonstrates her superior understanding of her profession and, at least temporarily, emerges superior to the demands of her social environment. She herself seems to be uncertain whether to pity the young couple or to be scornful about their entire way of life. She identifies more with the "Wife," whose capture she views as unfortunate, but on the whole she rises above the situation of her potential "Partnership." That her Governess, still expecting "great Things" of Moll, urged her to join with them suggests that uneasiness in their relationship that gives a certain edge to the genuine affection they feel for each other.

On a somewhat more complex level, the passage moves to a more general type of judgment. With this couple, partnership in crime is also a sexual partnership. Moll's Jemy never suggests that she join him in such a life. When he has to return to being a highwayman, he parts from Moll affectionately and leaves her behind. But these "Partners" share in everything, including the violent crime of "breaking open the House." It was this kind of crime that brought so much disapprobation on John Sheppard a few years later, for if the locks on a house were to be broken with such ease, who could be safe? The folly of the crime is a reflection of the levity of the couple, and if sad, their punishment is hardly surprising. And given Defoe's continuous metaphor of crime as a form of trade or business, this self-contained little narrative has larger significance as an illustration of all foolish partnerships in mad "Projects."

In speaking of the couple, Moll selects her words carefully, as if she wonders how much she should tell and how to tell it. Just as the "young Woman and a Fellow" do not add up to husband and wife but rather to "Partners," so they are not actually skilled thieves, and the vague partnership in unreal matters ends in their real hanging. Sensing their insubstantiality, Moll is tentative. For all the "help" of her Governess in this arrangement, she only agrees to a "kind of League," and she does not so much join with them in their crimes as allow herself to be "carried" into what she aptly calls "Adventures." The crime that leads to their capture is real in its circumstantial enumeration of the "3 Gold Watches," but the danger is so obvious that Moll merely arranges "a kind of an Appointment." She reports the failure of the scheme with some satisfaction and returns to her clever line on the relationship of the couple in sex, robbery, and hanging. Her final statement on the end of her "Partnership" has to be read as ironic, since she was never truly in anything resembling a relationship of mutual cooperation and trust. And the finality of her last statement has some of the quality of her farewell to the Colchester family with whom she left her children: "and that by the way was all they got by Mrs. Betty." Unfortunately for Moll, she is unable to say good-by to her Governess so effectively.

How many writers can lay claim to greater skill in narrative? Defoe carries his plot forward in time, develops Moll's character in her environment, gives us a vivid sense of the kinds of robberies that were occurring at the time, teaches the reader to worry about housebreaking while warning thieves and businessmen against foolish adventures and especially foolish partnerships. And all of this is accomplished while Defoe is both amusing us and giving us a slight chill of horror at the dismal end of the couple. Critics may talk of Defoe's "unconscious artistry," but of what use such a term may be in speaking of a combination of genius and a lifetime of experience in writing is difficult to comprehend.

Moll Flanders: Inside and Out

Michael M. Boardman

Commencing *Moll Flanders* . . . placed Defoe at a crossroads. He wanted to maintain the posture that he was only presenting the memoirs of another, in part because storytelling was not yet quite respectable, in part because he believed readers derived more benefit from accounts they believed true. More technically, his expertise, one might even say his faith, rested with the individual episode. The Puritan view of experience might well provide his stories with a kind of retrospective unity; but in the vital stirrings of the subject's own experiences, unity is an optical illusion resulting from the myopia of ego. The retrospective memoir reflects this chaos of life's flow while projecting, artlike, a sense of order and causality, even though that sense frequently in Defoe is a chimera.

Moll's book, then, is like what Roland Barthes calls a "lover's discourse." "Throughout any love life," Barthes reflects, "figures occur to the lover without any order, for on each occasion they depend on an (internal or external) accident. Confronting each of these incidents (what 'befalls' him), the amorous subject draws on the reservoir (the thesaurus?) of figures, depending on the needs, the injunctions, or the pleasures of his image-repertoire." The material of Moll's story falls into separate categories. Episodes could be classified according to whether they involve relations with men, or theft, or any other highly general category. They form a set of paradigms, like grammatical categories, on which Defoe can draw in order to maintain his vaunted "Variety." Yet, as Barthes says of the lover's dis-

From *Defoe and the Uses of Narrative*. © 1983 by Rutgers, the State University of New Jersey. Rutgers University Press, 1983.

course, "No logic links the figures, determines their contiguity: the figures are non-syntagmatic, non-narrative; they are Erinyes; they stir, collide, subside, return, vanish with no more order than the flight of mosquitoes." Just as the lover's musings are linked only by their presence in the mind of the same lover, and their sequential, though not patterned, existence, Moll's episodes appear, while we are trapped within them, to have the randomness of reported experience.

The analogy will finally break down, as will be seen. But for now, it is enough to show how this illusion of disjointedness has led to so many difficulties with the book. In her imperviousness to criticism, Moll seems much more like the opaque figure of a nouveau roman than she does the lucid and potentially understandable character of the traditional novel. Long after Moll, Robbe-Grillet was to object to the "heroes" of traditional fiction, the manipulated creations that, far more than Moll, came to dominate prose fiction. From Richardson and Fielding to Hardy and Conrad, characters had been "constantly solicited, caught up, destroyed" by their authors' value-charged rhetoric, "ceaselessly projected into an immaterial and unstable *elsewhere,* always more remote and blurred." They had been, for whatever purpose, employed by the creator, not allowed their own integrity.

Moll, like Robbe-Grillet's "future hero," remains "on the contrary, *there,*" oblivious to one's wishes, even to one's "commentaries." Moll is not *disponible,* or, depending on how one wishes to create narrative meaning, she is infinitely so. In one sense, the reader must generate her meaning, since Defoe does not. In another sense, following Robbe-Grillet's argument, the reader cannot "fill" Moll's interpretive spaces because Defoe has tried to leave no fissures in Moll's presentation. Those he has left—contradictions, for example—are inadvertant, nonfunctioning. Interpretation of her, therefore, begins to "seem useless, superfluous," if not, as Robbe-Grillet says of his "heroes," "improper." Defoe applies no such aesthetic, much less moral or ontological, absolute to Moll. Something else, reflected in the dust-devil swirl of conflicting theories about her, shuts off interpretation or renders it hopelessly indeterminate. In his preoccupation with the integrity of the single, verisimilar episode—Defoe's "thesaurus" of "figures"—he has replicated the local ambiguity of a real memoir. Moll, as ostensible memorialist, provides no more of a referential "framework" within which she may be judged than do Pepys or Boswell for themselves. The illusion of self-reference precludes her being seen, within her episodes, as a means to some end not contained within the circle of her own perceptions. She is a narrative exemplification of Gödel's Proof: there is no way to confirm or refute her being as long as the reader remains inside her system, her text.

The overall form of *Moll Flanders* does not emerge as an object of contemplation by the ordinary process of fitting part to part to derive a whole. Parts, like Moll herself, have edges that cannot be rubbed off. The entire story may have a meaning, but the significance of each episode results, as it does in the reader's experience of his own life's "episodes," from an act of individual will. The wiliest deconstructionist would strive to no avail— or perhaps to certain success—over Moll's text, both because there is no strong system and because no clear authorial intention emerges from episodes. One may step out of the book, as I shall argue shortly, and perceive an intention to conceal intention, which could then be deconstructed; but that is an infinite circularity, always self-confirming. If the illusion succeeds, the question of the intention of Moll's story should not arise, at least not from the diachronic flow of the episodes themselves. Moll comments on all things as she sees fit, What does her story comment on? Like the new novel, *Moll Flanders* attempts to affirm nothing, a nice paradox in itself. The reasons are different for Defoe and for Robbe-Grillet, of course. Assertion in the modern world is self-refutation. As Barthes says, "Everything I do has a meaning (hence I can *live,* without whining), but this meaning is an ineffable finality: it is merely the meaning of my strength." For many modern authors, assertion has become a joke on the self as well as on the reader. So the author withdraws for primarily ontological reasons, aesthetic ones following in their trail. Yet no one doubts that it is a new *novel* for which Robbe-Grillet and others have served as collaborative midwives. Defoe, on the other hand, distrusts not assertion per se, few writers having tendered more opinions on more subjects, but fiction that reveals by its patterned signification its own fictitiousness. He maintains the local inertia and silence of literal truth because to do otherwise would ensure that the overall fictional purpose became manifest page by page. He writes fiction he does not want to be experienced locally as fictional.

Yet Defoe's self-denial, or timidity, does not extend to the whole. It is doubtful, in fact, whether authors can, for whatever reason, withdraw far enough from their works to accomplish what Robbe-Grillet advocates, unless they are willing to pay a tremendous price. Even selection of what to represent implies choice, and choice implies value. Once it is understood that Moll's episodes have been selected according to a standard of refinement, one can see that the local illusion of factuality is itself illusory. The whole of *Moll Flanders* is judged to be a product of some intelligence other than Moll's without positive evidence of that presence being given within episodes. Two intentions are at work, and they do not "merge." *Moll Flanders* is a collection of episodes drawn from truthlike paradigms. Its syntax is clearly fictional. Many critics have felt this disjunctiveness without being able to explain it. It is implied in the common observation that Moll's odyssey could easily be lengthened, shortened, or rearranged, but that the book is nevertheless a novel. Defoe's old and well-learned reportorial skills must coexist with his growing desire to organize represented randomness into a whole that will reflect, if nothing more, the control of art. Episodic fragmentation, Crusoe's confused but mightily various ramblings, had brought credibility; the historicity of the *Journal* achieved an affective coherence. In *Moll Flanders,* Defoe sought ways to impose fictional form on materials that would still retain the superficial opacity of real events. As in most crossings of intention, the result is more difficult to analyze than the intersecting impulses. There is the liveliest sense of random variety in Moll's life. Yet one recognizes, after pulling back from the flow of story, just how carefully the illusion has been arranged. The product is a book that the reader experiences as a result of one semiotic system but can understand only by attending to another. As Walter Wilson said long ago, Moll's story is "an epitome," a compendium of the essential pleasures of autobiographical narrative, ones possible only intermittently in actual memoirs and diaries. Defoe makes his book a collection of such moments.

That such an unusual design does not approximate the later novel should be apparent. Defoe still refuses, as so many have argued, to judge Moll page by page, declining therefore to create *himself* as an internal, purposeful presence. Values and events do not fuse. At least the beliefs that give rise to this type of prose fiction do not, as they try to do in traditional novels, help in any discernible fashion to determine the local experience of the narrative. Defoe plays no omnipotent Intercessor, no Jehovah or Zeus, preferring instead the role of impersonal deity, presiding from afar. To meddle in his story contradicts all his old habits, as well as the underlying beliefs about storytelling with which he is either, as one chooses to see it, encumbered or blessed. Even so, once he has permitted some principle other than lying like the truth to enter in, he has at least taken a step toward creating his own presence in the story, even if, like Moll herself, it refuses to interpret its own existence.

With a few important exceptions that will be treated later, episodes in *Moll Flanders* retain all the conventional appurtenances of truth, as Rader has demonstrated. Cause and effect do not operate in any consistent fashion. Yet neither does one find the paradox of a consistent, causative principle of fortuity, as in *Tom Jones.* Seldom can the nature or quality of episodic closure be predicted, although there is indeed a principle of closure at work, to be examined later, because it is a part of the book's syntax but not present in any of the book's paradigmatic categories. The local premise of Moll's existence is that she acts as a natural person would act. These features of the book's individual episodes, and a few others, lead Rader to argue that the book makes full sense only if it is understood as a "simulated naive incoherent autobiography." Defoe intends to present "the incidents as if they were not invented but merely reported." Moll's aimless recitation, the lack of any "sense of full consistency either of psychological portraiture or implicit ethical judgment," her languid manner of relating sensational incidents—all indicate Defoe intended readers of *Moll Flanders* and his other first-person narratives to "construe" the "matter as real."

In addition to accounting for many of the commonly recognized local features of the text, Rader's hypothesis solves a number of critical controversies as well. For example, few critics of the book have avoided trying to account, in terms of the book's overall meaning, for the puzzling anomalies and discontinuities of the story and of Moll herself. She is not merely inconsistent. She seems ruled by no governing vision that would make a virtue even of inconsistency. What other critics see therefore as either novelistic confusion on Defoe's part—perhaps because the form is in its infancy—or thematic coherence—Defoe intends to present a picture of moral confusion—Rader argues is the natural consequence of imitating a true story. The adequacy of Rader's hypothesis finally depends on whether local effects produce an overall illusion of truth that of course would be at odds with the reader's external knowledge that the whole is a fiction. This question must wait until the texture of the episodes is examined.

Certainly much of Moll's attraction for readers lies in her evasiveness, her strange and frequently inconsistent strategies for dealing with a hostile world. One watches Moll as one watches his more interesting acquaintances, with a kind of puzzled fascination. No implied author helps to balance or reconcile her contradictions, her shifting mixture of assertiveness and indirection. She does not spring, it seems, from the same resources of imagination that spawned a Macbeth and would in time create a Clarissa and a Gwendolyn Harleth. Unlike Moll, these others exist so that one may finally come to understand and sympathize with their souls' confusions. Character, like every other significant element in a traditional dramatic or narrative action, serves as a complex set of signals indicating probable direction. Character, more importantly, serves as a constraint on meaning, on the reader's judgment. Clarissa's character does not exist for its own sake, although the success of the book does depend to a certain extent on the beauty of the finer brushstrokes. As a continuing and powerful semiological system, character both causes and results from complication, engendering both the basis of instability and the possibilities for its resolution. Moll's traits fail to become an intelligible "language," although because of their indeterminacy they can act as admirable departure points for any reader's private associational activities. Moll's personality therefore tends to float, to spurn any will to order inside her story. As a result, like the "future hero," Moll "may, according to the preoccupation of *each reader,* accommodate all sorts of comment—psychological, psychiatric, religious, or political." Yet, as an "indifferent Monitor," Moll refuses to yield to these "potentialities." Interpretation fails to explain Moll, in the root sense of "make flat" and therefore observable at a glance. It must rather stretch her, raise some of Moll and lower other aspects in order that she may fit the critic's mold. Some, of course, would argue that it is criticism's treachery to blame, and this is partially true. Even so, a few examples of significant disjunction will show that Moll herself is the source of both pleasure and critical confusion.

Two contiguous episodes will serve nicely: Moll's near arrest for a theft she did not commit and the subsequent theft of the horse. In the first instance, Moll is for once falsely accused, dragged into a shop, "kept by force," and "barbarously" used. Finally, some men who have pursued the real thief usher him into the shop. Recognizing a rare opportunity for a legal coup, Moll insists on appearing before a justice—a dangerous gambit, since her past exploits are so well known. The judge hears both sides, discharges Moll as the innocent party, and reprimands the accuser. He binds over the master and commits to Newgate the "Journeyman" who had most grievously insulted Moll. By "good Management," Moll and her attorney come off with "rather more" than two hundred pounds by threatening a suit. This is Moll at her calculating best, adroit at the risky business of concealing her identity and past while at the same time manipulating an experienced tradesman into fearing an action Moll dare not bring. Then, "in good Circumstances indeed," with seven hundred pounds in money and a cache of stolen goods, far more than she would ever need to live comfortably, she sets out "not long after" this affair dressed "like a Beggar." An ill-chosen disguise, the "most uneasie" she ever donned, her clothes make it difficult even to approach a "gull." Yet she does meet with a "little Adventure." A drawer asks her to hold a horse while he attends to his master. Moll "takes the Horse, and walks off with him very soberly, and carri'd him" to her "Governess." Moll herself sees the "Robbery and no Robbery"—she cannot sell the horse, or take it to a stable—as "Ominous and Threatning."

How is the reader to take it? The very quality of fabrication, of patterning, that Robbe-Grillet condemns in the traditional novel, its ability to impose on the reader the values of the author, would dictate, if one were in a novelistic world, that this discrepancy function as a purposeful signal.

Ordinary enough such moments may be in the real confusions of real people, nor is one often able to explain them. In the traditional novel disjunction must refer to probable developments. Take, for example, the most significant contradiction of a character like Lizzy Bennet: she prides herself on her discernment of character, recognizing immediately that Collins is unworthy both of her hand and her friend Charlotte's, yet she clearly forms too precipitously an unfavorable opinion of Darcy. Her good opinion of her own sagacity becomes therefore liable to shocking correction, leading to a deepened understanding of herself, and, within the comic probabilities of *Pride and Prejudice,* to a moral worthiness that then renders her a deserving candidate for fulfillment.

Moll's "muddle" seems at once to invite a simpler and demand a more complex response. Since the local experience of random truth is so powerful, one may accept as "like life" the juxtaposition of cunning with carelessness. After all, the most skillful confidence men are themselves sometimes "taken." One certainly cannot tell if irony is intended, unless one is willing to accept as "knowing" a conjecture about what Defoe "must" have believed. Were everyone the kind of naive, unanalytical reader Defoe probably thought he was writing for, one would probably respond with charmed but puzzled fascination, and go on avidly to the next episode. The history of the traditional novel interferes, however. As Ian Watt notes, two hundred years of reading authors "such as Jane Austen and Flaubert" who "incorporate such conflicts and incongruities into the very structure of their works" makes it difficult for any modern reader, even of the most plastic of imaginations, simply to "forget" the existence of a Defoe behind the mask. Defoe *must* intend to mean, as did later authors that are also called novelists. Indeed, I have suggested that the potential for allusive generalization residing in Moll's portrayal stretches so widely that few can resist its blandishments. Moll's confusion then becomes an indication of approaching doom, since she can no longer distinguish safe from dangerous criminal activities. Or Moll seems, on the contrary, no hardened reprobate precisely because of this harmless, unthinking, almost comic sally. Lacking any strong system of represented belief but with over two centuries of traditional fiction always bidding him to find meaning in inconsistency, the modern reader falls back on the last sanctuary of critical desperation: he creates the meaning he fails to find. Nourished on symbol and semantic complexity, yet thwarted by Defoe's literal paradigms, one must search elsewhere for what Defoe usually refuses to provide.

Except for obvious blunders, which are neither interesting nor critically significant, readers are prodded into repeated and various independent skirmishes with the text by these discrepancies and discontinuities. They range from clashes of episodes, as was just seen, to minor linguistic oddities. Almost as soon as one meets her, one may notice Moll's peculiar attitude toward the crime for which her mother was committed to Newgate. Moll says that her "Mother was convicted of Felony for a certain petty Theft, scarce worth naming, (*viz.*) Having an opportunity of borrowing three Pieces of fine *Holland,* of a certain Draper in *Cheapside.*" There is of course some doubt about the "Circumstances," so that Moll is uncertain "which is the right Account." This innocent passage presents virtually a model of the interpretive problems faced at every turn in *Moll Flanders.* How is one to judge Moll here? Some editors annotate "borrowing" to point out that Moll probably means, of course, "stealing." But that is little help. The diminutive force of "petty" and "scarce worth naming" clearly conflicts with the fact that what her mother stole was probably pretty valuable: *three* pieces of *fine* linen. If one imagines Moll as the writer of her own memoirs, spending the "Remainder" of her years "in sincere Penitence" with her dear "Jemmy," how can one countenance this casual attitude toward *meum* and *tuum?* "Borrowing" may now be used ironically to mean stealing, but I suspect most do not view the attitude as admirable, unless the act was indeed not stealing: "May I borrow a cigarette?" If Moll is not herself being ironic, what then becomes of her penitence? Or, is she indirectly condemning the brutality of a society that would punish with death such an objectively "petty" larceny? In that case, how does the message itself comment on Moll's later behavior? If the irony is Defoe's, at Moll's expense, then the sincerity of her repentance again is suspect. It would seem that the process by which an author's intuition becomes embodied in a form and then reproduced in the reader, as Croce describes it, has been blocked on both sides of the text. The reader can make all sorts of plausible conjectures about what Moll and her experience mean. Yet in doing so, it should be realized that one exercises powers authorized, not by the government of the text, but by one's individual right to create meaning where it literally does not exist.

Thus the "instruction" Defoe used to "Justifie the Publication" of Moll's "Private History" frequently has hard struggle to rise in our minds. Moll herself, of course, often points the lesson of her own behavior, but her "interpretations" of her own life are no more constrained than are her reader's. As moral geographer, she has abilities that are anything but awesome and her "muddle" has not escaped notice. It is easy to conclude that Defoe did not himself recognize the difference between an appropriate generalization and one seriously askew. But on one side of Moll is Crusoe and on the other Roxana. They do not always perceive their own inconsistencies, but when they do their remarks are usually perspicuous. Even so, for one so acute in her estimates of others, Moll's self-knowledge has wide gaps. For example, when she is still new in crime, Moll meets up with a little girl, leads her to a deserted passageway, encourages the child to prattle away, and steals her gold necklace. It occurs to Moll, as she stands there, to kill the child "that it might not Cry." She suddenly realizes that it must be "the Devil" who put into her mind this heinous thought, and she is so "frighted" by it that she is ready to "drop down." She feels what anyone, whose normal sensibilities had not been blunted by repeated acts of inhumanity, would feel. Yet there is no retrospective peroration of any kind on the horrors crime has led her to countenance. This "last Affair left no great Concern" upon Moll since, she says, "as I did the poor Child no harm, I only said to my self, I had given the Parents a just Reproof for their Negligence in leaving the poor little Lamb to come home by it self."

Whatever different values readers hold, they will still perceive something amiss here, a discrepancy not resolved by finding out that "casuistry" was a common deliberative mode in Defoe's time. No author steps in to reconcile the incommensurability of situation and commentary. Moll's "casuistry" is the problem, not the solution. Formally, a lively sense of personage may demand the juxtaposition of seemingly conflicting traits in order to suggest complexity. Yet complicating Moll, without any clear design to which complication is subordinate, tends to destroy the "simple" didacticism Defoe sometimes seems to desire. What is the "real" message of Moll's missing the deeper implications of her desire to kill? Is it that "Necessities" made her "regardless of any thing?" The convolutions of personality threaten to disappear beneath such "interpretation." Later writers would probably have tried to construct an instability out of these materials. Defoe is content to present them. One's judgment of Moll during such moments depends on no strong textual dictates, but on one's own differing naturalistic expectations about real people in the real world. One turns inward, if one questions Moll at all, for plausible explanations of her conflicting blindness and insight, since Defoe is silent.

The preface to *Moll Flanders* suggests that such moral ambiguity, the inadvertant result of writing an imitation of a true story, cannot have been intended in a book he asks readers to value more for the "Moral, than the Fable," the "Application" rather than the "Relation." Although the overall form of the book testifies to its fictionality, the continuing indeterminacy of episodes constitutes a liability a later novelist could not endure for a page. Perhaps no stretch of narrative is entirely free of redundancies, fissures, uncompleted thoughts, missed or ill-conceived designs, from all sorts of usurpations or deflections of the text's frail unity. Yet some novelists manage, by violence or cunning, to yoke their recalcitrant materials to a single purpose, the imposition of form on the fluctuating moments of experience. Moll's story has entirely different virtues, although many readers would not exchange her fascinating mutations for all of Fielding's benevolent and perspicuous tyranny. Nevertheless, whether one conceives of the novelist's art as sweetened communication or significant talespinning, something is lost when one cannot know how to judge Moll. Defoe, like the "new" novelist, pays the price no neoclassical author would willingly pay: an impairment of his ability to sway his readers' minds.

Even so, moral ambiguity in *Moll Flanders* does not equal an illusion of literal truth, equivalent to the *Memoirs [of a Cavalier]* and the *Journal*. All it indicates is an absence of any continuous controlling presence, one that functions on every page. Indeed, Moll and her story contain and exist in much that is negative space. Yet the book still manages to tell the reader that it is a fiction. "The one impossible event," Woolf says of Moll, "is that she should settle down in comfort and security." At any time that one can say something cannot happen in a narrative one is on the trail of a converse principle of generation and selection. What it might be for Moll's story cannot be seen until one examines in some detail the differences between the ways fiction and autobiography are conceived. The obvious answer is only partially satisfactory: first-person novels, no matter how closely based on actual events, are self-contained. As interesting as it may be to discover real people standing just behind Hemingway's characters, the reader does not have to know of them to participate fully in the experience and significance of the story.

Real memoirs and diaries, on the other hand, have a referential relationship to the events they purport to relate, even, paradoxically, if readers are not familiar with those events. For this reason is the power of the *Journal* historical: there must have been a 1665 plague in London. Perhaps all narrative finally involves illusion, since it attempts to represent something in words that is not itself words. It is known, however, that some kinds of narrative, satire for example, force the reader to construe their matter as referring outward. *Gulliver's Travels* is peremptory in this regard, at least in many passages. When Gulliver says that "Flimnap, the Treasurer, is allowed to cut a Caper on the strait Rope, at least an Inch higher than any other Lord in the whole Empire," the reader may not have the slightest inkling that for Flimnap one is meant to read Walpole. Yet the reader knows that Flimnap equals someone. That inference is necessary if the book is to be anything more than a charming bit of nonsense. This sense of reference, or representing something that has existed or yet exists in heaven or on the earth, is not automatically eradicated by the imposition on materials of an illusion of "madeness." Paul Fussell has noted just such qualities in First World War memoirs, and argues that it assimilates them to the novel. Rearrangements of chronology, transformations of events, manipulations of personae—all the devices of treatment as opposed to substance—may point to the gray area where fiction and history might meet.

But the intention to write neither novel nor memoir precludes such aesthetic accommodations. Since works that are easily recognized as one or the other are written with some regularity, something else must be involved. The distinction is precisely in use, the "for the sake of what" involved in all human productions. In the real memoir, decisions involving the "telling" are made for the sake of the subject, the "I," conceived of as the author's own public personality. Concealment, changes in the story's clock time, any sort of rhetoric, broadly conceived, occur to assist the memorialist in recording his own personality in words that convey his reality. The effect, although only to be achieved in the mind of a reader, is understood as an aspect of the writer. In the first-person novel, on the contrary, experiments with both matter and technique occur to realize effects conceived of as in the reader, although the novel's form is the sign system in which the potential effect is embedded. Anyone who has ever tried to write much fiction knows the radical difference between these two modes. The fabulist asks, among other things, not how better to reveal himself, but how to achieve the desired effect.

Yet this clear distinction is blurred by *Moll Flanders*. Defoe intends the local episode to be taken as the product of a naive diarist, while at the same time the overall form reveals a mimetic intention not Moll's. What signals authorship other than the narrator's is neither referentiality nor verisimilitude, but selection designed to make possible a continuum of pleasure and significance ordinarily available only sporadically in real memoirs. While the separate episodes contain an implicit request that the reader conceive of Moll as nothing other than the reporter of her own experiences, the book as a whole requires that one view it as an epitome. The book's positive fictional principle coexists, uneasily, with the firmest local sense of truth. The same anomaly is at work in *Robinson Crusoe*, but not in any systematic and purposeful manner. Sequences exist that give the strongest impression of elements specified for an effect, within an overall structure that imitates the expressive intention of autobiographical documents. What I have called novelistic moments in Crusoe's story, mimetic "outcroppings," will not easily be encompassed by a general expressive illusion. It is not surprising that Starr cannot make the autobiographical model he designed to explain the subsuming expressive illusion of *Robinson Crusoe* fit the virtually opposite relationship of episodes to overall intention in *Moll Flanders*. Now it can also be seen why Rader, working within a framework that assumes parts are subordinate to the whole, would emphasize the illusory expressiveness of the book at the expense of its qualities of purposeful design. One has seen too much fictional patterning, the other too little.

By his choice of what not to represent, Defoe signals that his heroine is indeed a creation and not the naive autobiographer that the reader's continuing encounters with her try to confirm. She never develops anything like the tight, causal relationships with other people that are necessary for the probabilities of the novel to occur. Even so, the potentialities for such an interlocking are frequently present, as in her first romantic involvement and her later doings with her "Jemy." It is of course not sufficient that she reencounters Jemy later on. Novelistic character requires that human interaction result either as a cause or an effect of a systematic narrative syntax. Given sufficient time and paper, Defoe could have had Moll meet up with everyone she had ever known before and he still would not have written a novelistic action—although some of the randomness of Moll's adventures would thereby have disappeared.

Her story progresses, rather, by a principle of avoiding such regularity. At any time she finds herself "the happiest Creature alive," she ceases, not necessarily to be interesting as a potential novelistic character, but as a chronicler of wondrous episodes no real memoir could ever match. Calm stability usually terminates abruptly and, for the story at hand, conveniently: "an odd and surprizing Event put an end to all that Felicity in a moment." Moll is left "the most uncomfortable, if not the most miserable" creature "in the World," all the more eligible for her next adventure. Defoe may even include a précis to call to mind just how delicious previous entanglements have been and therefore how much there is to look forward to: "Then it occurr'd to me what an abominable Creature am I! and how is this innocent Gentleman going to be abus'd by me! How little does he think, that having Divorc'd a Whore, he is throwing himself into the Arms of another! that he is going to Marry one that has lain with two Brothers, and has had three Children by her own Brother! one that was born in *Newgate,* whose Mother was a Whore, and is now a transported Thief; one that has lain with thirteen Men, and has had a Child since he saw me!" Periodically, the slate is wiped clean: "I was now a single Person again, *as I may call my self,* I was loos'd from all the Obligations either of Wedlock or

Mistressship in the World; except my Husband the Linnen Draper, who . . . no Body could blame me for thinking my self entirely freed from." Within a short time of marrying Moll, the new husband loses his money, then "grew Melancholy and Disconsolate, and from thence Lethargick, and died."

Defoe declines to represent stretches of secure happiness, but not because such scenes are not novelistically promising. The history of the traditional novel is in part the process of finding more and more of interest in just such "inert" moments of life. But *Moll Flanders* is not a traditional novel. It is a fictional refinement of real memoirs. Veritable chronicles of self can proceed by means of the same lopped episodes that Defoe employs, by means of extended analyses of the nuances of every moment, or, more commonly, by means of some unsystematic combination of the two. The paradox of Moll's story is that the quality of the next episode can always be predicted, with even more certainty than in the traditional novel, but the probable content can never be known. Whatever happens next in Moll's "life," it is sure to be sufficiently bizarre to hold the reader's interest: a kidnapping by gypsies; a seduction by one brother followed by marriage to the other; another marriage, this time to her own brother; marriage again, to a man who thinks Moll has a fortune, and leaves her, reluctantly, when he finds out she does not; the difficulties of a pregnant Moll, alone and husbandless—and on and on. Literal verisimilitude of the sort found in the *Journal* and the *Memoirs* requires the inclusion of an occasional episode that reasserts the reality of the life just by showing how uninteresting a full report of it can sometimes be. Moll's life is never intentionally unsensational, although her manner of relation frequently is.

Another important modification of the factual tradition, a refinement of possibilities present in *Robinson Crusoe,* does not force itself on the reader if local effects are examined: Moll's role as narrator. Of course, she is vividly represented, although her personality frequently changes in unexpected ways under the pressures of succeeding episodes. Her point of view, however, never deviates, a consistency she shares only with Roxana. Events are always seen through the central, pervasive "I," to a degree no mere pronoun can convey. Unlike Crusoe, Jack, and, it goes without saying, H. F. and the Cavalier, Moll never simply reports what she sees for its own intrinsic interest. She melts the world down and recasts it in the mold of her own personality. Crusoe, before and after his island isolation, recedes into the background in order to describe what in some ways never lost primacy: the world outside his mind. In such a narrative strategy, which is also a kind of authorial vision, experience is not conceived of as psychological and changing. It is a static "other," existing externally and therefore capable of being communicated only if the idiosyncratic self is kept from meddling. The future of the novel, quite obviously, waited behind other doors, to be unlocked only by discoveries leading to greater revelation of personality, not its muting. *Moll Flanders* is one such discovery, even though the ubiquity of the beholding consciousness is itself encompassed by the superficial illusion of truth. The advance had to be made, and some have equated it with the rise of the novel. Indeed, Moll seems so much more vivid than earlier narrators not just because of the much-praised paraphernalia of realism—many earlier pseudomemoirs used similar strategies of internal confirmation—but because Defoe refuses to dilute the intensity of her focus. Vividness is not, however, identical to the traditional novel.

Even at those moments when Moll seems to pull back and observe, her personality merely bides its time until it can integrate the scene into the internal landscape.

> One Adventure I had which was . . . I was going thro' *Lombard-street* in the dusk of the Evening, just by the end of *Three King Court,* when on a sudden comes a Fellow running by me as swift as Lightning, and throws a Bundle that was in his Hand just behind me, as I stood up against the corner of the House at the turning into the Alley; just as he threw it in he said, God bless you Mistress let it lie there a little, and away he runs swift as the Wind: After him comes two more, and immediately a young Fellow without his Hat, crying stop Thief, and after him two or three more, they pursued the two last Fellows so close, that they were forced to drop what they had got, and one of them was taken into the bargain, the other got off free.
>
> I Stood stock still all this while till they came back, dragging the poor Fellow they had taken, and luging the things they had found, extremely well satisfied that they had recovered the Booty, and taken the Thief; and thus they pass'd by me, for I look'd only like one who stood up while the Crowd was gone.
>
> Once or twice I ask'd what was the matter, but the People neglected answering me, and I was not very importunate.

If Moll seems here to be merely an observer, the context of the passage reveals something quite different. She has just robb'd the child of the gold necklace. She then goes on to say, "I had a great many Adventures after this, but I was young in the Business, and did not know how to manage, otherwise than as the Devil put things into my Head. . . . One Adventure I had which was . . . ," and then follows the scene I have quoted at length. After Moll's wry comment that she was not very "importunate," she continues, "but after the Crowd was wholly pass'd, I took my opportunity to turn about and take up what was behind me and walk away: This indeed I did with less Disturbance"—to her conscience, that is—"for these things I did not steal, but they were stolen to my Hand." This thinking involves the "casuistry" Starr finds at the heart of Moll's meditations, but it also displays the pervasive manner in which the external world is transformed by Moll's mind into corrolaries of her own hopes and fears. Moments of such connection are scattered throughout Defoe's narratives. Only in *Moll Flanders* and *Roxana* are they a unifying device, albeit an unobtrusive one. The traditional novel finally came to feed on such relationships, character implying event and the reverse. Even so, Moll's interactions yield no pattern, nothing of the ongoing and progressive synthesis necessary for the novel to come. The material is present, the technique would not now be a radical shift for Defoe, but yet no novelistic world emerges. Instead, Moll's story is a series of varying, fascinating portraits of the shifting landscape of a mind at work on the materials of survival.

The simplest test of this hypothesis would be to ask what response that Moll might make to her adventitious "Bundle" would seem inappropriate, given the book's internal geometry: leaving it out of fear; picking it up, but recognizing that her act was still theft; joyfully possessing it without even a consideration of the ethical question; or something else? No standard of exclusion within the book rules these or other possible responses anomalous, although any single reader might say, "No, that's not the Moll *I* know." The only "necessity" is that Moll link events to her psyche and situation. Her ubiquity provides an important building block for the house of the novel, but as yet there exists no blueprint.

I have been talking for the most part about the tacit experience that results from Defoe's duality of purpose, but the specifiable meaning of *Moll Flanders,* to the extent that it contains and does not merely suggest ideas, arises from this same source. Defoe's aim finally is ironic, though not in any ordinary sense. Within an overall structure based on the refinement of effects possible in true stories, he enfolds episodes that reveal enticing, often bewildering, ambiguity. As in the compound sentence, where either coordinate clause can precede, so too in *Moll Flanders* can local elements be rearranged, with no violence done to the overall structure. One half of this paradox does not challenge explanation. Although, as Stewart says, "illusion had become the sine qua non for aesthetic enjoyment of serious fiction" in the previous century, by the time Defoe writes, the necessity for the ruse had diminished. It is too strong to say that fiction had suddenly gained respectability; even in 1740 Richardson pretends he merely edits Pamela's letters. More likely, illusionists such as Defoe probably tired of the strong constraints the pseudomemoir imposed on experimentation. Little manipulation of the author-reader relationship, the source of so many innovations in narrative over the next two centuries, could be attempted when the narrator had to seem to be the author. The shift from event-centered narrative, no matter how many undetectable liberties Defoe might take with the materials of the *Journal* or the *Memoirs,* to the representation of personality was a drastic change, and one Defoe clearly did not always find palatable. Creation has a way of interfering with the didactic tidiness he says he valued. The Horatian ideal proves efficacious only when authors employ unambiguous, highly coded, even stylized forms to serve as carriers of lucid commentary, social or moral wisdom, as Johnson knew. The writer who essays a new species of writing risks not being understood, as novelists as diverse as Fielding, Sterne, Emily Brontë, Joyce, and Camus have discovered. It is no accident that Johnson attempted no realistic fiction in which the world, as in Moll's tale, is "promiscuously described." The mimetic impulse can run counter to Johnson's belief that "where historical veracity has no place," fabulists should represent only "the most perfect idea of virtue." How could an author like Defoe, who for so many years had thought of himself as a kind of public conscience, avoid feeling a certain uneasiness if a created personality began to take on life of her own?

At any rate, in outfitting Moll with a life and opinions, Defoe leaves behind all but the most commonplace of his own beliefs. With sufficient knowledge of his ideas expressed in other places, one can easily track Defoe in *Moll Flanders*. Moll quotes the "wise Man's Prayer, Give me not Poverty least I steal." As Starr discovered, Defoe argues the same view of necessity and crime in the *Review* and *The Complete English Gentleman*. Once Moll has been sentenced to death, she begins to "look back upon" her "past Life with abhorrence." Faced with eternity, it seemed "the greatest stupidity in Nature to lay any weight upon" this life. Again, as Starr notes in his edition of the book, Defoe has anticipated this otherworldly view in "A Vision of the Angelick World." On nearly every page, Starr finds Moll iterating Defoe. What is finally notable about this mass of opinions—Starr's *Moll Flanders* is the most heavily annotated Defoe narrative in the Oxford series—is that they could be of abiding interest only to the historian of moral commonplaces.

Few of Defoe's ideas are particularly dissentient or even original, certainly as contrasted with the innovation of his narrative experiments. Despite Novak's desire to show that Defoe has been unjustly "condemned for shallow content and a paucity of moral perception," he must finally concede that Defoe "was neither an original nor a profound thinker." It is undoubtedly distorting to single out, from a study that bases its conclusion on such an admirable breadth of reading, just one of Novak's examples: "Although Defoe's use of necessity [in *Moll Flanders* and *Roxana*] as an excuse for theft followed the theories established by the seventeenth-century civilians, his extension of this same doctrine to prostitution seems to have been without precedent." Neither shallow nor profound, one yet wonders how such stale ideologies could possibly be the cause of Defoe's continuing popularity. The history of ideas approach to Defoe seems to have left us with a pale, washed-out retailer of tired truisms, instead of the vital, engaged explorer of uncharted narrative ground I think Defoe was. The very facility with which Defoe's hackneyed opinions come tumbling out of Moll's mind indicates, not that they are the heart of the book, but that he assigns plausible beliefs to Moll at any point her personality seems to call for generalization. To argue, therefore, that "we cannot understand the morality of Defoe's 'moral romance' " if we have not painstakingly acquired "a knowledge of natural law"—or, someone might similarly argue, Defoe's political or economic ideas—seems to me special pleading, an implicit denial that most readers have a sound basis for their liking Defoe, as well as a drastic simplification of the often indirect ways belief can operate in narrative. After so many attempts to find semantic complexity in Defoe have turned up so little that is indeed complex, might it not be time to look elsewhere for his power to endear generations of readers?

Finally, since Defoe's unquestionable talent seemed to be storytelling, and since stories, by their very nature, mean as a function of their teleologies, the locus of Defoe's beliefs in *Moll Flanders* may be elusive if one pays overmuch attention to the inveterately conventional utterances of Moll herself. It is Moll's *story* that means, much more than her opinions, just as it is the working out, by coincidence, of Tom Jones's fate, rather than Fielding's ideas about the necessity for prudence in the world, that is the central meaning of Fielding's novel. As a creator of human situations, Defoe is far more profound than any of the separate ideas he assigns his characters. This disjunction indicates, of course, that Defoe has not yet evolved anything like a novelistic technique to subordinate belief to a system of character and action. Novak recognized the liability: "although Defoe's preoccupation with natural law enriches the content of his fiction, it also tends to destroy some of his excellence as a creator of character." Novak has it just backwards, I would argue: it is Moll's personality that "enriches" the triteness of the ideological content. Yet the relationship is, as Novak implies, additive.

One important problem in the study of narrative today is meaning, as so many European critics, like Todorov, fully understand. It may finally be understood, with the help of writers like Defoe, that meaning does not arise in a single way, as Sheldon Sacks suggested fifteen years ago. Perhaps the surest way to guarantee that the question of meaning remains unanswered is to continue to employ a critical method that assumes in author's beliefs can simply be extracted from what the characters say or inferred in some easy way from what they do. Defoe's fate, to be interpreted into triteness, perhaps awaits any author treated by such a method. The tough-minded Fielding, for example, can thereby be made into a kind of mild Sunday school teacher admonishing his charges to love one another better, if only one conveniently forgets that, within the world of *Tom Jones,* it is not virtue that is rewarded but luck. The even more inexorable Swift, in the hands of critics who ignore Gulliver's status as a device for ridicule, begins to sound like some "humane" satirist who disowns his narrator's final misanthropic vision. He really was insincere when he said, *"Mundum odi."* The very choice of how views will be incorporated into narrative often reveals more about an author than the beliefs one can "pull" from the living texture of the story, a lesson Conrad should long ago have taught everyone. The enduring power of *Moll Flanders* resides, not in its messages, but in Moll's existence. She, and Defoe's other narrators, despite their social and legal transgressions, recommend all the conventionalisms of polite society—trade, monarchy, property, public morality—and of the spiritual life—faith, grace, God's mercy—with an explicit confidence hardly mystifying. One needs such beliefs in a society such as Defoe's, which cared little for the dignity or even safety of the individual.

So the formal paradox implicit in the structure of *Moll Flanders* extends to its meaning as well, since the conventionality of Defoe's heroine is belied by the kind of story she tells. Defoe had once said, "Mankind are Rogues by Birth." Yet that easy homily, inherited, as Novak says, from the tradition of natural law, had long since been superseded by a bitter personal knowledge, learned in betrayal, in hiding from friend and foe alike. The chaos of human relationships is of course reflected in the episodic subject matter of the book, but it also controls the episodic manner of relation, the refusal to subsume the confusion to any strong system. The formal development of his narratives, the movement from loose pseudofactual structures in which he embodies his more general and less powerfully personal ideas to more novelistic teleologies, is paralleled by a growing desire and ability to represent the chaos from which he had suffered. The "refinement" of *Moll Flanders,* in which such moments of noncommunication are not only collected, but prevented from casting mutual light on the surrounding ones, mirrors the attempt to make sense of the world that is in part the story of Defoe's narrative development. This is not to commit the "fallacy of imitative form" or the "ancient reductive fallacy of identifying the thoughts of characters with those of their author," of seeing Moll, Jack, and Roxana as just so many projections of Defoe's personality. Almost the opposite is true. Defoe stands back from Moll and creates her whole. Yet, even though she is a product of his imagination, and not of an act of impersonation, he has not achieved the same thing as an immanent presence that would make of his beliefs, especially his less sanguine ones, positively functioning elements. The discontinuity of human life is implied by the disjunctions of *Moll Flanders,* but it is not literally represented; the form is not imitative of his profound beliefs. Not until *Roxana* will he find a way to manipulate the materials and techniques of fiction so as to create traditional novelistic meaning, or what will become traditional long after he is dead. The moral indeterminacy of Moll, as expressive as it is, took Defoe away from the traditional novel.

Crime and Comfort

Ian A. Bell

The main process of the narrative is Moll's convoluted and twisting search for comfort and security. She originally, and innocently sees the path to stability lying in her own honest efforts as a worker, but, as one critic [John J. Richetti] puts it, "what Moll will have to learn to do in the course of her narrative is to relinquish this middle-class dream of honest and self-sufficient survival." It is very interesting that, whereas *Crusoe* showed the possibilities of self-sufficiency, *Moll* shows the impossibilities. Moll lives in a social world, and her attempts to secure stability are disrupted as much by her relationships with other people as by accident or chance. Of course, it may be tempting to see her presentation of this as an attempt at excusing herself, but her character is never as fully motivated and understood as that would require. Whatever the case, the agency of her disillusionment is her romantic life, and the book balances the tale of Moll the criminal adventuress with the Moll who presents herself as the helpless victim of uncontrollable desires. In the later half of the book, these two tales seem rather at odds with one another, but there is little conflict in the earlier part.

Moll's first romantic encounter is with the elder brother of the family she is living with, and it is described in such a way as to allocate the tale to the group of romances about rakes and innocent serving wenches. Moll has already been established as a simple, rather gullible girl, and the seducer is introduced characteristically and conventionally as a rake:

> a gay Gentleman that knew the Town, as well as the Country,
> and tho' he had Levity enough to do an ill natur'd thing, yet had

From *Defoe's Fiction*. © 1985 by Ian A. Bell. Croom Helm, 1985 too much Judgment of things to pay too dear for his pleasures; he began with that unhappy Snare to all Women, (*viz.*) taking Notice upon all Occasions how pretty I was.

The endangering feature here, presented as familiar to all readers of this sort of fiction, is Moll's innocent vanity. The whole episode is presented without dramatic impetus, as though it is recognised by readers as inevitable, and it is understood in purely conventional terms. Moll affirms "my Vanity was the Cause of it," and the whole episode has a rather stylised, impersonal appearance to it. The most important thing about it is not the loss of Moll's virginity, which she is characteristically coy about, but the awakening of insight that it produces. At one point, Moll overhears a conversation between her future seducer and his sister, in which he praises Moll's merits. The sister replies in a very worldy and disdainful way:

> I wonder at you Brother, *says the Sister; Betty* wants but one Thing, but she had as good want every Thing, for the Market is against our Sex just now; and if a young Woman have Beauty, Birth, Breeding, Wit, Sense, Manners, Modesty, and all these to an Extream; yet if she have not Money, she's no Body, she had a good want them all, for nothing but Money now recommends a Woman.

The sister's sense of the supremacy of money, anticipating *Roxana*, is largely confirmed by the events of the tale, but Moll never comes fully to this cynical view. Readers are being alerted to the cynicism of the tale's world, but, very interestingly, the narrator does not participate in this all but universal sourness of view. Moll's innocence is damaged by her encounter with the rakish elder brother, but it is never fully dispersed. Defoe uses it to keep the book out of the category of pornography, where the heroine is as cynical as everyone else, and yet he is able to incorporate crime and promiscuity into a largely blithe narrative.

In fact, the issue of love and money was a recurrent theme throughout Defoe's non fiction, as well as appearing in *Colonel Jack, Captain Singleton* and, dominantly, in *Roxana*. It figures prominently in *Religious Courtship* and *The Complete English Gentleman,* and some critics have suggested that Defoe himself was heavily involved in discussing such matters when haggling over the dowry of his daughter Sophia. It would be possible to present the conflict between love and money in any fictional mode, and in non fiction, it appears often as tragedy—brief tales are given of foolish lovers, whose impecunity drives them to grief. However, in *Moll* it is kept in the comic mode by Moll's undying innocence. One critic claims that the book shows Moll's education in the ways of the world—"she learns that charm, wit, grace, and beauty are insufficient assets to the gentle world, but that diamonds are a girl's best friend." No doubt this view accurately represents the social world of the narrative, but Moll herself never becomes fully hardened to it as so many writers suggest. In the early part of the novel, she seems uncertain about her role, and makes very few recriminations of herself or others. She seems to accept the seducer's behaviour as being the way of the world, and her own innocence as being equally involuntary. The behaviour of the younger brother, who falls in love with her, at least maintains the possibility of conduct motivated by something other than money, and it helps to maintain Moll's naivety for a surprisingly long time.

Though Moll does recognise the power of economic necessity, it is by no means the only force which motivates her conduct or impedes her progress towards comfort. As her first seduction is completed, and the seducer gives her more and more money, Moll paradoxically announces her own culpability in the affair. She does not see the opportunity for her own self-advancement, and becomes in effect a willing, self-castigating accomplice to his scheme. Eventually, when he gives her a hundred guineas, she says, "I made no more Resistance to him, but let him do just what he pleas'd; and as often as he pleas'd." The money she receives is not understood by Moll as a bribe, but as an earnest of his sincerity, and as a confirmation of his good faith. Despite the financial reward, she does not seem to realise, even retrospectively, that her body and charms are marketable assets, though she is tacitly engaged in selling them. She sees the loss of virginity as closing down her economic options, rather than as opening them up, as it were— "for from this Day, being forsaken of my Vertue, and my Modesty, I had nothing of Value left to recommend me, either to God's Blessing, or Man's Assistance." It is clear that Moll is not scheming to entrap the elder brother, and that she still clings to the foolish notion that virtue is more saleable than vice. Even in retrospect, she does not qualify her view that love is a source of jeopardy rather than comfort, and that it enfeebles her pursuit of stability.

It is at this point that the narrative is complicated by the younger brother Robin's announcement of his love for Moll. Obviously, this serves to involve her in a grim dilemma, in which her emotional security is at odds with her financial stability. Is she to accept the love of Robin, which may entail his being cut off from his family, and rendered destitute? Or is she to stay secretly with the elder brother, and enjoy a covert but profitable affair? For a ruthless narrator, like the narrators of the Spanish picaresque novels, there would be no dilemma. The affair with the elder brother could continue while the marriage to Robin was contracted and carried out. Moll's situation is rendered complex, not by moral qualms, but by her irrational sense of attachment. Her individuality, which is made much greater than Crusoe's, is expressed by her emotional idiosyncracies, and this aligns her to the romance heroines of Aphra Behn rather than to the criminal narrators. She even goes so far as to say to the elder brother, "I had much rather, since it is come to that unhappy Length, be your Whore than your Brother's Wife." Her distresses cause her to fall ill, and she is diagnosed by the physicians to be "IN LOVE." She still seems to maintain a romantic conception of her affair, though the reader is surely invited to see it as a purely carnal and financial matter on the part of the seducer, who is clearly prepared to pay to get her off his hands. Eventually, she accepts his ending of the affair, and marries Robin. Since this alliance is neither romantic nor criminal, it does not appear in the narrative, and has as little force as Crusoe's marriage. We are told only that for five years they "liv'd very agreeably together," until Robin dies, leaving Moll "a Widow with about 1200*l.* in my Pocket."

All in all, this whole episode serves to bring into the novel the powerful force which Moll later refers to as "*that Cheat call'd* LOVE." Moll's view of romantic attachment is initially very unusual in context, and only gradually becomes sour. Defoe's professed views were rather different, and they too can be seen as idiosyncratic. In the context of contemporary debate, Defoe's arguments about romantic love, and its relation to matrimony, can be seen as fairly liberal. However, he still saw that the danger of romantic attachment was that it was often merely a screen for sexual desire, and that marriage based on sexual attraction "brings madness, desperation, ruin of families, disgrace, self-murders, killings of bastards, etc." Moll herself never develops any coherent attitude or policy towards her dilemma, and that is one of the ways she is rendered individual, distinct from conventional heroines and from Defoe himself. When describing her early sexual conduct, the retrospective Moll makes very few reflections, as though some of her illusions remain intact. In the preface, the "Editor" excuses this part of the book by claiming that it "has so many happy Turns given to expose the Crime, and warn all whose Circumstances are adapted to it, of the ruinous End of such Things, and the foolish Thoughtless and abhorr'd Conduct of both the Parties." Though the editor points out the moral lesson to be drawn, Moll does not, and the narrative does not seem to invite any such solemn reading. Moll's comments are very limited and never seem as strict as the editor would have us believe. Though she may recognise the shoddiness of the elder brother's behaviour in "shifting off his Whore into his

Brothers Arms for a Wife," she retains her blinding affection for him. She may retrospectively acknowledge that love is a cheat, but she seems helpless to prevent it, and her condemnation affects her behaviour negligibly.

Significantly, Moll does not interpret her treatment as a cruelty, and she does not become hardened against the world as the *pícaro* does. Love is understood as the area of Moll's life most subject to hazard, and it has the narrative function that the weather has in *Crusoe*. The tempests which disrupt the narrative in *Crusoe* are actual; in *Moll,* they are metaphorical, but nonetheless effective as agents of disruption. Moll may fall in love at anytime, though she does become much more self-assured as the book progresses, and there are the attendant hazards of children and illness. Yet though this area of her life is the most subject to chance, it is the area where Moll's moral scruples are most active. If the book presents itself as divided into criminal adventures on the one hand, and romantic interludes on the other, Moll saves her piety for the latter, and even there it actually does very little. In her criminal adventures, her self-reproach is infrequent and perfunctory, though there may be some signs of the pattern of overreaching apparent to the reader. Only in her romantic adventures does she offer any descriptions of evil, or show genuine repugnance or abhorrence, although in that area of her life she seems least responsible for her own behaviour. It may be suggested that what emerges in the narrative is a picture of what Lawrence Stone calls "the growth of affective individualism," placed within the context of a society which is hostile to such individualism, and within a narrative which relies more heavily on conventions and types.

Moll's self-assurance and calculation increase rapidly after the first marriage, and become the motivating forces for her second wedding. As she puts it, "I was resolv'd now to be Married, or Nothing, and to be well Married, or not at all." However, even within the self-imposed limits of caution and prudence, Moll is characteristically impulsive and excessive in the way she treats her husband's money, and in the way she thinks of love. She learns that life in London is very different from life in the relatively rural Colchester, a fact which was already apparent to the reader in the fast behaviour of the elder brother:

> I was not to expect at *London,* what I had found in the Country;
> that Marriages were here the Consequences of politick Schemes,
> for forming Interests and carrying on Business, and that LOVE
> had no Share. or but very little in the Matter.

Though Moll does come to accept the general truth that "Money only made a Woman agreeable," and that good looks and wit were good properties in a mistress, not in a wife, she still thinks of herself as an exception. Certainly, none of her marriages really deserves to be called a "politick Scheme." They all may start from that idea, but they are soon changed by foolishness or affection. She is persistently impolitic in spending money so easily, and especially so in paying attention to her feelings for her Lancashire husband, the fellow criminal Jemy. They extent to which her dealings are dominated by calculation may be surprisingly less than she herself believes. One critic claims that "Moll has to set aside many feelings and attitudes which she cannot afford . . . Moll lives a life crowded with event and absolutely bare of feeling." While it is clearly the case that Moll's life is congested, it is surely a mistake to think of her as devoid of feeling. There are even a number of occasions when feeling wins out over prudence, such as the incest and abortion episodes, and these typify her affairs more than does cynical calculation.

The very important episode concerning her unwitting incest is one of those instances of rediscovered family that appear throughout Defoe's fiction. The reunion between Friday and his father, Jack's rediscovery of his wife in Virginia, and Roxana's furtive reunion with her daughter are all used as central plotting devices in their respective tales. There are a number of these events in *Moll,* notably the meeting of Moll and her highwayman husband in Newgate, but the most important one is her discovery that she has inadvertently married her own brother. The event is her third marriage, and before entering it, Moll has satisfied herself that her spouse is after more than just her cash, Moll then briskly arranges the financial matters, and on this occasion, talks very little about romance. After they have settled in the husband's plantation in Virginia, Moll spends sometime with his mother, whom she realises with horror to be her own mother. Moll's first reactions are very dramatic and powerful:

> I was now the most unhappy of all Women in the World: O had the Story never been told me, all had been well; it had been no Crime to have lain with my Husband, since as to his being my Relation, I had known nothing of it.

Were she *only* to be concerned with financial security or comfort, she could accept this accident reasonably calmly, and could tolerate the living arrangements. But Moll repeatedly asserts that her position is somehow deeply repugnant to "Nature." Though she cannot be held in any way responsible for this state, which is the result of pure chance (and, on a narrative level, rather implausibly abrupt chance), she still suffers extreme guilt and shame. This alone would indicate that her life is not "bare of feeling," though the feelings may seem to be histrionically expressed.

Moll's secrecy about her incestuous marriage lasts a startling three years, a period of time more suitable to the fairy tale than to the realistic report. The truth eventually slips out in a quarrel, and her brother/husband is shocked into serious illness. One critic sees in this illness a parallel to Moll's own sickness before her partly incestuous marriage to Robin. Indeed, the two episodes can be presented as closely related—Moll's illness is interpreted as a kind of punishment for her deceptive marriage to Robin. Certainly, Moll herself has thought of the earlier marriage as incestuous, since she thought of Robin's brother while lying with Robin. There is a long casuistical tradition in which lustful thought are no less evil than lustful deeds. Of course, Moll herself makes no mention of any parallel between the two episodes, but that alone does not rule out its validity. Defoe could be said to be surreptitiously unifying his narrative by giving the reader a more coherent view of events than the narrator has, and so turning the narrator into an ironically myopic figure. Such a procedure would be wholly outside the realm of popular fiction, but it is still a possibility. However, the basis for such an analysis of the book's hidden structure is rather unconvincing.

The episode with Robin and the later marriage are only very loosely and chronologically related. Moll's three years of reticence has no parallel with her earlier, brisk behaviour, and generally the incest episode stands on its own, obtruding from rather than cohering with the rest of the tale. *Moll* is, of course, not the only eighteenth-century narrative to encompass incest—it appears, fleetingly, in *Tom Jones* and elsewhere—and Stone's book makes it clear that the whole subject was obviously under widespread discussion. Given the congested accommodation in which most people lived, and the lack of social mobility, acts of incest must have been frequent, though almost always covert. However, the idiosyncratic thing about the episode in *Moll* is the extent to which the narrator's revulsion is developed. Moll describes her feelings acutely and at some length:

> I was really alienated from him in the Consequence of these Things; indeed I mortally hated him as a Husband, and it was impossible to remove that riveted Aversion I had to him; *at the same time* it being an unlawful incestuous living added to that Aversion; and tho' I had no great concern about it in point of Conscience, yet every thing added to make Cohabiting with him the most nauseous thing to me in the World; and I think verily it was come to such a height, that I could almost as willingly have embrac'd a Dog, as have let him offer any thing

> of that kind to me, for which Reason I could not bear the thoughts of coming between the Sheets with him.

It is made clear here that the revulsion is not simply a kind of moral condemnation ("I had no great concern about it in point of Conscience"), but a kind of irrational, personal revulsion. The very graphic image of the dog enhances the power of Moll's remarks, which do not seem to fit easily into her otherwise rather blithe personality.

The horror which incest holds for Moll is reinforced by her lover's reaction to the discovery. He is so disturbed that he makes two attempts at suicide, and eventually falls into a consumption. This would indicate that Moll is not the only one to feel such powerful reactions, and gives the episode an eerie, frighteningly sombre effect. Yet the reaction is certainly given great dramatic force, by being so much greater than the audience might be likely to expect. M. E. Novak has shown that the condemnation of incest here is much stricter than would be likely from any of the theorists of Natural Law, from whom Defoe drew so much. The theorist Pufendorf, for instance, accepted that some countries might sanction incest, and that any European revulsion at it might only be the result of ingrained custom. Even the customs of the time were much less severe than Moll's reaction might lead us to believe. Lawrence Stone describes the legal position:

> the punishments meted out by Church courts in cases of incest in Elizabethan England were surprisingly lenient, and there is no reason to think that sodomy and bestiality were more repugnant to popular standards of morality than breaking of the laws of incest, which must have been common in those overcrowded houses where adolescent children were still at home.

If this was known to be true of Elizabethan courts, it is likely to have been the case in the 1650s, when, by the chronology of the tale, Moll's actions are alleged to have occurred. Bearing all these facts in mind, Moll's reaction to the incestuous marriage is highly dramatic, and unrepresentative of the way incest was treated in other popular discourses.

The episode serves in the tale to introduce a more thorough delineation of a character's responses to hardship. In *Crusoe,* the narrator's responses to privation were stylised and conventional. In *Moll,* much more of the narrative is taken up in presenting how things felt, and in rendering them immediate. To some extent, this makes *Moll* much more a book about character and development, though the development it portrays is fairly rudimentary. But Moll herself certainly has more than a conventionally unifying function. She is provided with qualities of individuality which keep the book's generic categorisation at bay. Because Moll is somewhat volatile and unpredictable, readers are unable to assimilate the full process of the narrative in advance, and so Defoe is able to move from the criminal tale, to the confessional or romantic tale, without having to change the conventional attributes to his narrator.

Another example of Moll's individuality can be seen in the way she responds to children. Much has previously been made of her rather casual attitude to them, though Stone has shown how common her type of "fostering-out" was, and though they are understood best as mere narrative props. After all, the narrators of *Moll*, *Colonel Jack* and *Captain Singleton* are all originally children discarded by their parents. However, it is worthy of note that Moll has curiously strict views about abortion. At one point, she is likely to bear a rather inconvenient child:

> my Apprehensions were really that I should Miscarry; I should not say Apprehensions, for indeed I would have been glad to miscarry, but I cou'd never be brought to entertain so much as a thought of endeavouring to Miscarry, or of taking anything to make me Miscarry, I abhorr'd, I say so much as the thought of it.

Seen in terms exclusively of self-interest and policy, Moll would be well advised to seek abortion. Her rejection of that recourse seems both irrational and fundamental, but not the result of deliberate thought. She rejects both abortion and incest on emotional, instinctive feelings of repugnance, not on the basis of some ethical code.

So far, then, Moll has been given a sporadically individuated characterisation, with eccentricities and idiosyncracies of viewpoint which cannot simply be explained as forgetfulness on the part of the author. Her motivation stems episodically from her sense of gentility, from her desire for economic self-sufficiency and from love. As such, it is much more varied than Crusoe's repeated "wandering Inclination," and his fears of death. Moll's behaviour is not made coherent (or even presented *as* coherent) by any series of references to the shaping hand of Providence. Nor does her criminal career fit into any obvious pattern of punishment or reward. The intensity of her emotional reactions makes Moll a much more complex character than Crusoe, and allows the narrative a greater flexibility than the more schematic presentation of the earlier tale. Crusoe's emotions were often presented, but only on occasions of guilt or loneliness, which could always potentially correspond to a providential reading. Moll's emotions are much more extensive and varied than those of her generic predecessors, like Lindamira, and they certainly rely a lot less on the alleged promptings of supernatural intrusion. Even her conscience does not seem to be a very important factor (despite the attention drawn to it by the preface), and her emotions are largely spontaneous and unpredictable.

In her criminal adventures, Moll fits more readily into the acknowledged fictional patterns of her predecessors. The narrative occasionally takes on the pattern of the confessional tale, with the apparently penitent Moll expressing conventional disapproval of the former conduct with which her narrative is actually trying to entertain us. She sees most of her thieving as voluntary, and so has to see herself as culpable, though throughout the presentation of this part of her life there is a great deal of elision and equivocation. She believes that her earliest crimes arose from necessity, and, therefore, that they are conventionally acceptable. They serve to warn the reader that anyone can be driven to such extremes, and to remove the taint of prurience from reading by fitting the thefts into an admonitory pattern. She is aware that theft can sometimes be acceptable as an alternative to starvation, but even this rudimentary moral point is presented imperceptively and sporadically.

Necessity is offered as an exculpatory plea on a number of occasions. Moll deceives most of her suitors about her true financial position, for instance, and offers the excuse that such deviousness is necessary for an unprotected woman in a hostile world. The degree to which Moll is genuinely in jeopardy, and the degree to which she is a predator in her own right, are kept uncertain throughout the narrative. However, Moll's view is that such crookedness is necessary, and if it is necessary, then it is morally excusable. Such a view is consonant with Natural Law theory, and appears throughout Defoe's fiction. Her reliance on necessity as a plea of justification is most prominent when she is in difficulties, and when she is discussing her affairs with a banker:

> I was now a loose unguided Creature, and had no Help, no Assistance, no Guide for my Conduct: I knew what I aim'd at, and what I wanted, but knew nothing to pursue the End by direct Means; I wanted to be plac'd in a settled State of Living, and had I happen'd to meet with a good sober Husband, I should have been as faithful and true a Wife as Virtue it self cou'd have form'd: If I had been otherwise, the Vice came in always at the Door of Necessity, not at the Door of Inclination.

If this position were plausible, then Moll would always be in the clear, and the fact that it sounds so much like arrant self-justification may turn the narrative more towards irony when Moll is being reflective. Moll's attempts to excuse her lapses are never fully convincing. Her greatest criminal excesses arise much more from the fear of eventual or impending poverty than from immediate or imminent poverty. She steals in advance of necessity, in case necessity comes along, which is as morally incoherent as retaliating before provocation.

Though we need not fall for Moll's interpretation of her own life, we are still invited to follow the events avidly, in an involved way. In the narrative, as opposed to Moll's moral interjections, the theme of exculpatory necessity recurs. The banker describes his estranged wife as "a Whore not by Necessity, which is the common Bait of your Sex, but by Inclination, and for the Sake of Vice." Moll's acceptance of this tale helps her justify her own behaviour, and she does consistently approach other people's behaviour in very simple graphic terms—acting from necessity is excusable, but acting viciously from inclination is reprehensible and intolerable. It is noticeable that this view of inclination is very different from Crusoe's where it was partly an exculpatory factor in itself. However, even this very simple moral view within the tale, which is the kind of graphic morality necessary for the functioning of popular fiction, is disrupted whenever emotional attachment intrudes. She never applies her standards to the elder brother in Colchester, to her mother, or to Jemy, and so the narrative, it seems, takes only a fitful and crude interest in the moral status of its events.

Moll's first criminal acts occur after her banker husband has died, leaving her very poor. She is led to quote a remark which becomes familiar in this book, as well as in *Colonel Jack* and *Roxana,* "Give me not Poverty lest I steal." Another familiar tactic is her attribution of her criminal inclinations to the Devil's promptings. Certainly, this is the first time in the narrative that Moll offers a supernatural intervention, and it does seem to happen at a disquietingly convenient time:

> This was the Bait, and the Devil who I said laid the Snare, as readily prompted me, as if he had spoke, for I remember, and shall never forget it, 'twas like a Voice spoken to me over my Shoulder, take the Bundle; be quick; do it this Moment.

Moll's dramatic presentation of her own state is less conventional than Crusoe's and more aware of itself as a piece of imaginative reconstruction. The use of a sly "as if" renders the account dramatic, and yet makes it also appear as though Moll is the victim rather than the aggressor here. As a presentation of the supernatural, it should not be taken seriously. Even in *Crusoe,* the talk of predictions, dreams, "secret hints" and so on, was never fully sustained or coherent, but it was persistent enough to become an integral part of the narrative, and to assist in its generic categorisation as sporadically a spiritual autobiography. In *Moll,* the reference is too isolated for this, and serves to concentrate attention on the drama of the moment, rather than on any overall plan.

Moll's life of crime is by now established, and in this respect the narrative becomes somewhat uneasy. The mode of presentation is never simple or single, and many passages offer ironic possibilities, as well as admonitory ones. In the famous episode where Moll justifies, or attempts to justify, the theft of a child's necklace, the variety of modes is obvious. If we accept the Natural Law background to the tale, then stealing from someone worse off than yourself is clearly wicked. However, Moll retrospectively tries to make the theft into an act of rough charity and benevolence, in a charmingly flagrant piece of rationalisation:

> Poverty, as I have said, harden'd my Heart, and my own Necessities made me regardless of any thing: The last Affair left no great Concern upon me, for as I did the poor Child no harm, I only said to my self, I had given the Parents a just Reproof for their Negligence in leaving the poor little Lamb to come home by it self, and it would teach them to take more Care of it another time.

Once she has cast herself in the role of protector of innocent children, Moll is captivated by the notion. The child's mother obviously suffers from "Vanity," and the maid whom Moll supposes to have been looking after the child becomes "a careless Jade . . . taken up perhaps with some Fellow that had met her by the way." This kind of expansive opportunism is typical of Moll's presentation of her criminal life. The quickness of thought, and recognisable consistency of character, is very much more pronounced than it ever was with Crusoe. Defoe makes use of the opportunities of the criminal narrative to incorporate comic capers, and to establish a consistently self-seeking character for his narrator.

So both Moll's career as a thief, and as an autobiographer are best characterised by spontaneity and opportunism. Rather than being carefully planned and organised by Moll, both careers are erratic, wayward and skilful in the exploitation of opportunity. It is possible to think of Moll psychologically, unlike Crusoe, and to see her as consistently impulsive, cunning and volatile. Consequently, Moll's narration is much less stable than Crusoe's, and she seeks to encompass even more forms and modes than he did. The various conflicts and discrepancies in *Crusoe* could not be explained by the character of the narrator, but they can be more readily explained that way in *Moll*. Moll consistently offers us *her* view of the world, rather than simply being used to present a generically competent view of the world.

Such an argument comes close to claiming that the book is consistently ironic, and that reading it depends on the reader's sceptical aloofness from the narrator. However, there is no need to make the book quite as consistent in viewpoint as that. When discussing the episode of the child's necklace, and a later outrage where Moll takes advantage of a drunken gentleman (for his own good, as she says), Dorothy Van Ghent came to this conclusion:

> We are left with two possibilities. Either *Moll Flanders* is a collection of scandal-sheet anecdotes naively patched together with the platitudes that form the morality of an impoverished soul (Defoe's), a "sincere" soul but a confused and degraded one; or *Moll Flanders* is a great novel, coherent in structure, unified and given shape by a complex system of ironies.

What Van Ghent might mean by a "complex system of ironies" is not clear, and the alternative views she suggests are surely not the only possibilities of articulating the text. It seems fairer to suggest that the book is a collection of anecdotes, some of which would find a home in scandal-sheets (why not?), but that the characteristics of its narrator give it the kind of shape it has. At times, too, an ironic reading is made possible by the tension between what Moll tells us, and what we can deduce from her omissions and distortions. However, the book is too eclectic to be understood as consistently ironic or consistently mimetic. Its modes are various, as are its genres, and the sole consistency lies in the emergent character of the narrator.

The self-serving nature of Moll's narration can be seen by looking at the way she refers to the supernatural. In *Crusoe*, the narrator had nothing to gain by invoking Providence, only an increase in guilt, and yet another threat, so his references to it were not self-serving. However, Moll's use of the plea of necessity, and her supernatural motives, becomes much less convincing as the tale progresses:

> Thus the Devil who began, by the help of an irresistible Poverty, to push me into this Wickedness, brought me on to a height beyond the common Rate, even when my Necessities were not so great, or the prospect of my Misery so terrifying; for I had now got into a little Vein of Work, and as I was not at a

> loss to handle my Needle, it was very probable, as my Acquaintance came in, I might have got my Bread honestly enough.

The return of the ideal of working diligently at a small skill is only cursory, and Moll returns to grand acts of theft. There is some sense here of the limits of excusable behaviour, as there is in the incest and abortion episodes, and, in a much more dramatic way, in *Roxana*. However, the most important thing about the passage is the way it signals to the reader that Moll is now exactly the kind of gentlewoman she wished to be at the very beginning. Moll herself does not draw any parallels, and this may indicate a larger organisation of irony than is often apparent. The references to the Devil as the force which prevents her from attaining this sought-after quiet life seem highly unconvincing and conventional, but show Moll herself trying to fit her criminal behaviour into a recognised generic pattern. She wants to present herself as the paradigm of the good person locked in combat with the Devil, losing temporarily, but winning finally. Our recognition that her behaviour does not fully accord with this pattern is strengthened if we are familiar with the popular genres in which it is apparent, such as the confessional tale, and the spiritual autobiography.

The book is entering into a kind of ironic parody of these popular genres, by laying great emphasis on Moll's reticence, and her partial disclosures. In the overt, stated interpretation of her life, Moll moves from childish innocence, into poverty, justifiable theft and unjustifiable theft, before finally being rewarded for her penitence. Clearly, if it is possible to have doubts about any stage in this process, it is possible to doubt the probity of her penitence. Like the early storm repentances of Crusoe, it seems very much in the penitent's interests, and to be motivated entirely by fear. It occurs after Moll has returned to Newgate, and is haunted by her fate. She has been caught red-handed in the act of theft, and has been condemned to death. Her tutor in crime, too, has been condemned to die in prison, and the combination of shocks and frights brings Moll round to a kind of temporary penitence. She had been provided with further admonitory examples—like the arrest of two colleagues, or the sight of a thief being given over to "the Rage of the Street." Even in court, when she was seeking damages for her wrongful arrest, her earlier bravado prevailed. The significant date of Christmas Day, on which she was arrested, passed without comment. After all these warnings, more apparent to the trained reader of confessional tales than to the narrator, she finds herself in Newgate. In M. E. Novak's view, these episodes are most properly seen as unnoticed examples of stealthy Providence. In discussing Moll's behaviour after her first casual attempt at repentance, at the fire, he says, "it is suggestive of divine Providence that the next time Moll attempts to steal at a fire, she is struck and almost killed by a mattress which is thrown from a window." However, the possible providential pattern before her capture is not mentioned by Moll herself, and seems only fortuitous.

Moll's subsequent "conversion" is made to seem easy and brief, and it has no effect at all on her behaviour. In the oppressive atmosphere of the prison, she feels what she takes to be stirrings of remorse and abhorrence for her past life. The sight of Jemy, also imprisoned, makes her feel irrationally responsible for his fate. There is no need for this, and it seems like emotional indulgence. Jemy was, after all, a confirmed and notorious highwayman before meeting Moll, and he had simply returned to his old occupation. Once again, we are not obliged to accept Moll's understanding of events, and the brief possibility of irony is again present. She is still under sentence of death, and the language she uses to express her contrition makes it all seem very self-interested:

> He visited me again the next Morning, and went on with his Method of explaining the Terms of Divine Mercy, which according to him consisted of nothing more than that of being sincerely desirous of it, and willing to accept it; only a sincere Regret for, and hatred of those things I had done which render'd me so just an Object of divine Vengeance . . . I was cover'd with Shame and Tears for things past, and yet had at the same time a secret surprizing Joy at the Prospect of being a true Penitent, and obtaining the Comfort of a Penitent, I mean the hope of being forgiven.

The paradoxical simultaneous occurrence of shame and joy is typical of the moment of conversion, as represented in Defoe. However, Moll seems to get the shame out of the way fairly quickly, and to get on with the joy as soon as possible. She seems struck by "Divine Mercy" as a kind of bargain, and her references to its "Terms" makes the idea of a transaction more apparent. This stress on the convenience of penitence, and on its cheapness, must make it seem like just another violent transition in the narrative, rather than the ultimate, important one.

Moll's conversion seems as naive and impulsive as all her earlier behaviour. Its self-interest is much more apparent to readers than to her. When she tells it, she is not trying to deceive us into thinking it to be more serious than it really was. Rather, she is consistently expressing her eagerness and whimsicality, which she thinks of as earnestness and conviction.

This curious kind of persistent innocence is one of the book's most interesting features, and one which moves it out of the adventure category into the character study, at least in parts. The innocence is apparent not only in the conversion scenes, but also in the passages of self-justification, such as the theft of the child's necklace. Moll is emphatically not trying to put one over on us, or to get away with things she believes to be wrong—she simply believes anything that strikes her at any moment. Her most idiosyncratic feature as a criminal narrator is her lack of guile, and her credulity, which is a kind of unworldliness very much at odds with her aggressive criminality. Rather as some people may be tone deaf or colour blind, Moll seems to be morally insensitive to her own behaviour, and to remain somehow remote from its implications. This allows her to change with great speed and agility, and yet also to avoid cynicism and hypocrisy. She understands events spontaneously and irrationally, as in the abortion scene, and never finds an overall view of herself. Though it would be very wrong to think of her as an *ingenue,* she does seem to lack any wholehearted calculation, and retains a freshness and spontaneity to the end.

Such openness to change can be seen in the way Moll eventually does get out of Newgate. Her more worldly fellow prisoners advise her that bribery is the way to secure freedom, and Moll is convinced. It takes little argument to get her to see that lining pockets is a more reliable and immediate way of having her sentence commuted than prayer. As her tutor says, "did you ever know one in your Life that was Transported, and had a Hundred Pound in his Pocket." Moll's ready acceptance of this advice shows the degree to which her conversion is simultaneously genuine and self-seeking. It is adopted as the best way to escape hardship, and as such, it is seen to be a full, if not a profound, emotional experience. It cannot be seen as a moral experience, since it is dispersed as soon as an easier, or quicker, avenue to escape is revealed.

It seems, then, as though Moll's conversion might be wholly genuine as long as it lasts, for Moll is entirely convinced by it. The fact that she does not retrospectively assess its impermanence is very interesting, and shows us something about the conventionality of the narrative posture. At this point in the tale, Moll has not only bribed her way to a reprieve from the gallows, she has also gained a kind of conditional pardon. Though she takes no direct part in the bribery herself, she is certainly prepared to accept the intercessions of others on her behalf, and does not inquire at all closely into their methods. It would be inappropriate to see this as hypocrisy, because of Moll's suddenness of emotion. It may appear inconsistent at first, but once Moll is seen to be volatile and persistently changeable, it seems an appropriate thing for her to do. We are not being invited to respond to this shift morally, but to accept it dramatically as one of the urgent transitions on which popular narrative is organised. These transitions are not deeply laid within the text, but arise suddenly, without premeditation.

Moll's penitence soon passes, and no memory of it lingers. The advantage of her abruptness is that it renders the past null and void, and Moll only exercises her memory as narrator, not as character. Once she has secured her release from Newgate, there are no vestiges of penitence left. When she sets up home in Virginia, she is perfectly prepared to live from the earnings of her criminal life, and even when she is reminded of her bigamous and incestuous state, she does not feel the need to do anything about it. Her money ensures a good trip to Virginia, and by bribing the ship's captain, Moll and Jemy are allowed their freedom very readily. At this point, stable and secure, Moll reminds us of her alleged purpose in writing her autobiography.

> As the publishing this Account of my Life, is for the sake of the just Moral of every part of it, and for Instruction, Caution, Warning and Improvement to every Reader.

But would every reader be instructed, cautioned, warned and improved by the narrative? The demands seem very great, and do not seem to accord with the narrative as it stands. The reader is likely to have been enthralled and entertained, as readers of popular fiction are entitled to be, but no other major endeavour has been noticeable. Popular narrative has the dual function of reminding you what the world is actually like, while allowing it not to be effective for a while. In *Moll,* the world is seen to be wholly mercenary and fairly vicious, as it is in *Crusoe,* but the potentially disastrous consequences of that violence are kept at bay by the conventional structure. *Moll* becomes a comic narrative, because of the self-preserving romantic innocence of the protagonist, and because that innocence is allowed to triumph.

"Out of the Jaws of Destruction"

Virginia Ogden Birdsall

Because Moll Flanders belongs almost exclusively to a city environment, the similarities between her experiences and those of Robinson Crusoe on his island and Captain Singleton on his land and sea journeys may not at first be obvious. Moll's is a social world—a world of competition, of buying and selling, of sexual encounters, of urban crime. Yet whatever the differences in form between Moll's adventures and those of Crusoe and Singleton, the essential content is much the same. Again, Defoe concerns himself with human psychology at its most elemental. As with Crusoe and Singleton, life for Moll is a power game. And the game, Defoe again recognizes, is in the final analysis a losing one.

But there is one way in which Moll resembles Crusoe not at all. If he is, at certain times on his island, *homo domesticus,* she is almost never *femina domestica*. She does, it is true, live briefly by her needle, but for the most part the background against which we view her is an outdoor one—the outdoors of the streets of London. The impression she leaves us with is one of virtually perpetual motion—seeking somewhere to go, moving toward some prey, running away from real or imagined pursuers. And even if her feet occassionally come to rest, her mind never does. It is forever working ingeniously on stratagems for survival, whether those stratagems have to do with devising tricks to trap a husband or coming up with schemes for thievery or defending her behavior before judges and other potential punishers either human or divine. In fact, there are times when some de-

From *Defoe's Perpetual Seekers: A Study of the Major Fiction.* © 1985 by Associated University Presses, Inc. Bucknell University Press, 1985.

vious escape route she describes is at once followed by an equally devious reasoning process, which she pursues with astonishing mental agility. In both kinds of peregrination necessity is the mother of invention.

To begin a discussion of Moll with perhaps the least debatable thing about her, however, is to begin with an area in which she resembles Crusoe closely. Like him she fears for her own physical survival with an intensity that rises many times to something close to animal terror. That Defoe himself understood this feeling well is amply attested to by something he once wrote in the *Review:* "I tell you all, gentlemen, in your poverty the best of you all will rob your neighbor; nay, to go farther . . . you will not only rob your neighbour, but if in distress you will EAT your neighbour, ay, and say grace to your meat too." London is for Moll a jungle in which a person must struggle to eat and must take constant precautions against being eaten. The opening pages of the story she tells establish the pattern. At her birth in Newgate, she is as effectually alone in the world as is the "newly born" Crusoe on his island, and is "kept alive" she knows not how. "I had no Parish to have Recourse to for my Nourishment in my Infancy," she writes. But by the age of three she is already moving toward adeptness at surviving, and after a brief interlude with gypsies, she is "taken up by some of the parish officers of Colchester" and contrives "to be provided for"—albeit the "Provision" is only "a plain Diet."

Fewer than three years later, however, she is once again without "so much as Lodging to go to, or a bit of Bread to Eat" and is "frighted out of [her] Wits." And we witness the same fears at the time of her involvement with her Bath gentleman: "I was not without secret Reproaches of my own Conscience for the Life I had led . . . Yet I had the terrible prospect of Poverty and Starving, which lay on me as a frightful Spectre, so that there was no looking behind me." Thereafter, her fear of starvation—in the literal sense at least—disappears from the forefront of her consciousness, only to reappear some forty years later, at the time of her banker husband's death. Then she finds her circumstances to "reduc'd" that she feels "desperate" and describes the "want of Friends and want of Bread" as "a desolate State." On the occasion of her first theft, she does give some "tormented" thought to her victim's possibly being "some poor Widow like me, that had pack'd up these Goods to go and sell them for a little Bread for herself and a poor Child," but she admits that soon "my Distresses silenced all these Reflections, and the prospect of my own Starving, which grew every Day more frightful to me, harden'd my Heart by degrees."

Moll can never be entirely "easy" unless she knows her present and future food supplies to be assured, and we find her still hounded by the same preoccupations about food as she arranges things on shipboard in preparation for being transported. The only details she mentions about the cabin are, significantly, that it had "very good Conveniences to set our Chest, and Boxes, and a table to eat on." And in anticipation of the voyage, she has, she says, "order'd . . . abundance of things for eating and drinking." What Eric Berne says of Robinson Crusoe is equally true of Moll: "The main problem is to have now all you want to eat and the indefinite assurance of future nourishment to avert the danger of starving to death." Crusoe, in his *Serious Reflections,* defines eating and drinking as "the main end of life" for human beings. That is, he says, "their enjoyment, and to get food to eat is their employment," and sometimes the process includes "their eating and devouring one another."

Moll, of course, knows all about this. When she remarks of the ship's captain that he was not a "Man craving and eager to make a Prey of us," we are reminded that she has, almost from the start, consciously inhabited a predatory world. Her experience with the older brother of the Colchester family has long since taught her how it feels to fall prey to someone. He had, she says, "known as well, how to catch a Woman in his Net, as a Partridge when he went a Setting"; he had "baited his Hook and found easily enough the Method how to lay it in my Way." Thus it is that Moll learns how easily women can fall victim to masculine appetites. But she is also quick to learn that the fed can be turned into the fed upon.

Meanwhile, she has learned another truth the hard way—namely, that the preying male may lust not after a woman's body but after her bank account. She again finds herself "catched" in a "snare" at the time of her second marriage—having, she discovers, "sold" herself to a fortune-hunting tradesman. And again she learns her lesson well, for from this point on, whenever she must enter the marriage market—a market which, as she says, "runs very unhappily on the Men's side"—she arranges to become the victimizer before she becomes the victim. In fact, when she takes up thievery, preying becomes her primary means of livelihood. She has clearly subscribed, by this time, to Rochester's conviction that in a knavish world only fools are good.

It is understandable, then, why Moll's tone, like Crusoe's, often hints at the self-glorying of the survivor and the controller, and why the cautionary advice she frequently hands out is almost always tinged with an undertone of condescension toward those who allow themselves to be taken advantage of. She insists, for example, that women seeking husbands have "Reason to be wary, and backward" and advises them to "act the wary Part." Self-protection is her motto, and she concludes by saying, "as for women that do not think their own safety worth their own thought . . . I can say nothing to them, but this, that they are a Sort of Ladies to be prayed for among the rest of distemper'd People; and they look like People that venture their whole Estates in a Lottery where there is a Hundred Thousand Blanks to one Prize." In Moll's view, only those who remain sharp-witted and are perpetually on their guard can expect to prosper.

And Moll has also learned, early in life, certain home truths about serving others. She tells us that the "service" her first love renders his younger brother "was not indeed done to serve him, but to serve himself," and she concludes, "so naturally do Men give up Honour and Justice, Humanity, and even Christianity, to secure themselves."

Later, Moll recounts the story of her faithful nursing of her Bath gentleman during his serious illness—"hazarding my Life to save his." But it is significant that this way of characterizing her service is not hers but his; it is what "he called it." For Moll, the "service" she renders is simply a sound investment, for not only does it elicit from the gentleman a gift of fifty guineas, but it brings his "deep Protestations of a sincere inviolable Affection." In view of all this, it is difficult to see how any reader could regard Moll as "warm-hearted."

Be that as it may, however, there can be little quarrel about what motivates her. We can say "greed." We can say "acquisitiveness." But from a Hobbesian point of view, Moll is simply looking out for herself in a typically human way; and if there is a certain boastfulness in her cautioning everyone else to do the same, there is also a substratum of wholly human fearfulness and insecurity.

In serving others, Moll is taking out insurance policies—like Robinson Crusoe before her. Consider, for example, her machinations on behalf of the captain's wife early in the novel. "My Dear and Faithful Friend, the Captain's Wife," she observes, "was so sensible of the Service I had done her in the Affair above that she was not only a steddy Friend to me but . . . she frequently made me Presents as Money came into her Hands, such as fully amounted to a Maintenance." And when, toward the end of the story, she presents her son with a gold watch (a stolen one, of course), she reports that "He took it, kiss'd it, told me the Watch should be a Debt upon him, that he would be paying, as long as I liv'd."

With reference to the question of service, what she truly wants, it seems clear almost from the outset, is total self-sufficiency. Hence her outspoken resistance as a child to "going into service" represents an instinctive longing for independence. While Robinson Crusoe on his island has no choice but to live by his "Finger Ends," Moll actively makes that choice—

the choice "to get my Bread by my own Work." The condition of servitude is anathema to her. After all, any state of dependency includes a certain helplessness. Moll can understand perfectly Jemy's "apprehensions" about being transported to Virginia, where "he should be the most ignorant helpless Wretch alive." But she can offer him reassurance: "I TOLD him he frighted and terrify'd himself with that which had no Terror in it; that if he had Money, as I was glad to hear he had, he might . . . avoid the Servitude supposed to be the Consequence of Transportation."

Moll, like Jemy, wants desperately to achieve and maintain a station in life above that of the "wretched Crew" of convicts. Jemy tells her "that Servitude and hard Labour were things Gentlemen could never stoop to," and Moll speaks later of their being "in the despicable Quality of Transported Convicts destin'd to be sold for Slaves." For them, to be a gentleman or a gentlewoman is to matter, to count in the world—to stand above the "ordinary Passengers, who Quarter'd in the Steerage" and even farther above their "old Fraternity" who "were kept under the Hatches . . . and came very little on the Deck."

Thus for Moll it is not enough simply to avoid servitude. She must "live great and high" as well. Not only is it important to her that Jemy be made to "appear, as he really was, a very fine Gentleman," but the outward trappings of a gentleman must include servants. Moll duly notes as part of the cargo sent from England both "a supply of all sorts of clothes" and "three Women Servants, lusty Wenches." Not content with feeling in control of her own life, she must feel that she controls the lives of others. She knows, with Hobbes, that servants are indices to the power of those they serve.

What is more, Moll loves making fools of people, proving them less clever and hence less powerful than she. And to recognize this is to see at once that her capacity for self-aggrandizement includes piling up not only money but triumphs in the game of power politics. There is no mistaking the relish with which she recounts every incident in which she succeeds in outwitting an adversary—and the worthier the better.

Moreover, it is a notable fact that the only two men in her life for whom she professes love are her first lover (the older brother of the Colchester family) and Jemy, both of whom prove a match for her in their talent for manipulation. Jemy—that man of "Vigour and Courage" whom she numbers among "the greatest Spirits"—is, for Moll, a power figure and thus a hero to be looked up to and at times served because he can save. ("'Tis something of a Relief," she says, "even to be undone by a man of Honour, rather than by a Scoundrel.") He is, however, a power figure whom Moll ultimately outgrows, as she comes to learn the limitations of the power he wields. "I was," she says at the time of her reunion with her son, Humphry, "as if I had been in a new World, and began secretly now to wish that I had not brought my *Lancashire* Husband from *England* at all." But then she does a little knocking on wood, as she quickly adds, "that wish was not hearty either, for I lov'd my *Lancashire* Husband entirely, as indeed I had ever done from the begining; and he merited from me as much as it was possible for a Man to do."

What both the older Colchester brother and Jemy possess, like Moll herself, is the ability to think clearly—to be the masters rather than the victims of circumstances. Moll's contempt for those who allow their wits to become befuddled is obvious. Thus she calls the "poor unguarded Wretch" whom she meets at Bartholomew Fair "a Fop . . . blinded by his Appetite" and asserts: "There is nothing so absurd, so surfeiting, so ridiculous, as a Man heated by Wine in his Head and a wicked Gust in his Inclination together; he is in the possession of two Devils at once, and can no more govern himself by his Reason than a Mill can Grind without Water . . . nay, his very Sense is blinded by its own Rage. . . . Such a Man is worse than Lunatick." And similarly, she tells later of stealing a gold watch from a lady "who was not only intollerably Merry, but as I thought a little Fuddled.

But in losing one's head one stands to lose a good deal more than a gold watch. One stands to lose one's very self, as Moll has long before learned. "His words," she says of her Colchester lover when he first begins to pay her attention "fir'd my Blood; all my Spirits flew about my Heart, and put me into Disorder enough." And although, as she says, "I soon recover'd myself," the recovery is short-lived, for in the next paragraph she reports: "my Head run upon strange Things, and I may truly say, I was not myself." It is clear then why, when she falls into a "Distemper" and becomes "Delirious and light Headed" after her lover's rejection of her, the phrases *oppress'd my Mind, agonies of my Mind, distress'd in my Mind, and my Mind was oppress'd* follow one after another within the space of three paragraphs.

For Moll as for Crusoe, moreover, devils of irrationality can threaten not only from without but from within, alienating one from one's true self. Moll, of course, ascribes her taking up and her continuing in her life of crime to her falling into a trap laid by the devil. "I am very sure," she protests, "I had no manner of Design in my Head, when I went out, I neither knew or considered where to go, or on what Business; but as the Devil carried me out and laid his Bait for me, so he brought me to be sure to the place, for I knew not whither I was going or what I did." Feelings of helplessness merge with feelings of confusion and lostness: "I cross'd and turn'd thro' so many ways and turnings that I could never tell which way it was, nor where I went . . . my Blood was all in a Fire; my Heart beat as if I was in a sudden Fright. . . . I still knew not whither I was a going, or what to do." Only when she ends up, at last, in Newgate, does she begin "to think." And as she goes on to remark, "to think is one real Advance from Hell to Heaven. All that Hellish harden'd state and temper of Soul, which I have said so much of before, is but a deprivation of Thought; he that is restor'd to his Power of thinking, is restor'd to himself."

Newgate is for Moll "an Emblem of Hell itself"; the "horrors of that dismal Place" fill her with such "terror" that, as she says, "I look'd on myself as lost." Speaking of "the hellish Noise, the Roaring, Swearing, and Clamour, the Stench and Nastiness," she associates such chaos with her own confusion of thought, which "left me overwhelm'd with Melancholy and Despair." Newgate is Moll's "Island of Despaire," and there, she tells us, her association with "a Crew of Hell-Hounds" brings it about that she "degenerated into Stone," turning "first Stupid and Senseless, then Brutish and Thoughtless, and at last raving Mad." The word *degenerated* or *degeneracy* appears three times here in as many paragraphs. She has, in her own view, become subhuman. She has, as John Richetti says, been "brought to accept death." She has virtually lost "the Habit and Custom of good Breeding and Manners" which have defined her in her own self-regard as a "gentlewoman," as someone who counts. "I was, I may well say I know not how; my Senses, my Reason, nay, my Conscience were all a-sleep." Degeneracy has "possessed" her to such an extent that all her "uneasiness" has disappeared—the fear of chaos, the sense of its horrors that has defined her humanity.

Robinson Crusoe never sinks so low, but then he has not begun life in Newgate. He has occupied the "middle Station" to begin with, while Moll has had to climb out of the dirt and darkness of a world where people are more *bête* than *ange*. Robinson Crusoe's Muscovite prince, in defining human life, speaks of "the Jayl of Flesh and Blood" the human soul "is now enclos'd in" and of "the Dirt and Crime of human Affairs"; and for Moll Newgate is that "Jayl." One of the things she commends in the "good Motherly Nurse" who first takes her in is that she is "Very Housewifly and Clean" and that she keeps ten-year-old Moll "very Neat" ("and if I had Rags on, I would always be Clean"). And when, toward the end of her career as a thief, she once adopts the disguise of a beggar-woman, she calls it "the most uneasy Disguise to me that ever I put on," since, as she explains, "I naturally abhorr'd Dirt and Rags; I had been bred up Tite and Cleanly."

Moll likes things to be neat and clean in every sense of the phrase. She shares with Crusoe a passion for order. Dirt, confusion, disorder are all equally threatening to her sense of command. They are equated with hell, with evil, with death. Thus, like Crusoe, she is easy and comfortable only when she feels she has life under control. Crusoe delights in being king on his island; Moll speaks of having "reigned" in the criminal world of London. Crusoe savors his powers of largess in his dealings with the African savages, who have, only a little earlier, constituted a threat to his life; Moll speaks pleasurably of her queenly generosity toward the journeyman whose testimony has threatened to send her to Newgate. "I abated his Cringes," she says, "told him I forgave him, and desir'd he might withdraw, as if I did not care for the sight of him, tho' I had forgiven him."

Again like Crusoe, Moll has the artist's instinct for imposing form on the content of her life. She refers to picking pockets as an "Art" and earlier expresses distaste for the methods of some of her criminal confreres, making reference to their "Course and unhandy Robberies" and deploring the fact that they get "into the House by main Force" and remarking with disapproval that they "broke up the lock'd Place where the Watches were." Not for Moll such lack of subtlety. She is an artist at her trade, and in recounting her successes, she implicitly compliments herself again and again on the ingenuity of her maneuvers. It is superiority of mind and not brute force that wins the day. People who use their heads come out ahead.

All of which leads us to recall that for Moll power is central. And if power resides in knowledge, it also resides in the money that a person of superior wit is able to accumulate. Here—at the money nexus—we can see many of the threads of Moll's seemingly complex personality coming together to form what is really quite a simple pattern. Moll's hatred of dirt and her love of money are the children of a single parent. Defoe seems to have known intuitively what Norman O. Brown was the first to articulate as an essential truth—that money, far from being, as Freud had argued, equated with feces, is a "*denial* of feces, of physicalness, of animality, of decay and death."

No wonder that Moll is horrifed by "the Stench and Nastiness of Newgate." It is, as she says, "the Place . . . where I was brought into the World" and the place that she has been seeking all her life to transcend. Commenting, as earlier noted, on having "scarce retained the Habit and Custom of good Manners," she goes on to bemoan the fact that "so thoro' a Degeneracy had possess'd me, that I was no more the same thing that I had been, *than if I had never been otherwise than what I was now*" (italics added). She has sought to rise above her origins—to deny the immutable fact that she was born, to quote Swift, "in the place of excrement"—and that she was born to die. And thus it is that she is appalled to discover "how Hell should become by degrees so natural and not only tollerable but even agreeable."

In the event, it is not God but money that is responsible for her being able to distinguish herself from the other Newgate wretches. "I had," she says, "obtained the Favour, by the help of Money, nothing being to be done in that Place without it, not to be kept in the Condemn'd Hole . . . among the rest of the Prisoners who were to die, but to have a little dirty Chamber to myself." And only money can raise her, once she arrives aboard the transport ship, above those "ordinary Passengers who Quartered in the Steerage" and her "old Fraternity . . . kept under the Hatches." As she has written long before, or rather etched on the window of her chamber, "*Money's Vertue; Gold is Fate.*" Ostensibly, Moll is here acting the role of the cynical realist, but in fact she largely lives her life on this conviction. To be without money is indeed to be "reduc'd"—to be denied "a settled State of *Living*" (italics added). "I knew," she says at one point, "that with Money in the Pocket one is at Home anywhere."

Money is not for Moll an end in itself but a means to the end of ease and comfort in the most elemental sense—a means of achieving a feeling of at-homeness in the world and of freedom from fear. She is an accumulator because money is power and lack of it is weakness and vulnerability. Invariably, Moll's estimate of her own value at any given time relates directly to the value of her possessions. Thus, when she returns from her first journey to Virginia, she dwells insistently upon how "little" she owns: "what little I had in the World was all in Money, except as before, a little Plate, some Linnen, and my Cloaths; as for Houshold stuff I had little or none, for I had liv'd always in Lodgings; but I had not one Friend in the World with whom to trust that little I had." Hence, in her own mind, she becomes a helpless prey. "If this Woman had known my real Circumstances," she says of her fellow lodger in London, "she would never have laid so many Snares and taken so many weary steps to catch a poor desolate Creature that was good for little when it was caught."

Very seldom, however, does Moll find herself at so low a point as this. Obsessed with accumulating "stock," she devotes all her ingenuity to the piling-up process. And here we have come back, in a roundabout way, to Moll's primitive, eat-or-be-eaten outlook on life. What she does, in Ruskin's words, is to "take dust for deity," as men have ever done. She is the archetypal human creature who has, as Norman Brown says, "confused excrement with aliment" and who "draws no distinction between the necessary and the superfluous." She insists, more than once, that whenever she behaves other than virtuously, "the Vice came in always at the Door of Necessity, not at the Door of Inclination." Knowing well the value of "a settled Life," Moll gives herself up to a pursuit of it, never seeing that "the Terror of approaching Poverty" will always lie "hard upon [her] Spirits."

But she does come close to a consciousness of her own drivenness when she is in the midst of her triumphs in the thieving line: "tho' by this jobb I was become considerably Richer than before, yet the Resolution I had formerly taken of leaving off this horrid Trade, when I had gotten a little more, did not return; but I must still get farther, and more . . . a little more, and a little more, was the Case still." She has kept hoping, she tells us, "that I might perhaps come to have one Booty more that might compleat my Desires; but tho' I certainly had that one Booty, yet every hit look'd towards another."

Moll expands her stock as compulsively as Crusoe expands his fortifications; the accumulating instinct drives her on and on. Not only do we find her listing her assets at the beginning and the end of every adventure, but all her life she remains an obsessive counter and keeper of accounts. "I told the Guineas over and over a thousand times a Day," she says, after she receives her first substantial payoff from her Colchester lover. And she refers to his "thousand protestations of . . . sincerity," "his thousand more preambles," "his many protestations," and tells us that he "kissed me a thousand times and more I believe and gave me money too."

Since it is Moll's accumulating tendencies that have drawn the most attention from critics of the novel, it is here that we must begin to come to grips with one aspect of that endlessly debated question as to Defoe's ironic intent in the novel. Of Defoe's treatment of Moll, Kenneth Rexroth writes: "He permits her to record her life only on the cash register, and in so doing he judges her without mercy." In espousing such a reading of the novel and of Moll's character, Rexroth is following the lead of Dorothy Van Ghent, who has insisted that either we must see Defoe's characterization of Moll as consciously ironic or we must regard Defoe's own value system as so corrupt as to invalidate his novel as a meaningful work of art.

Even if we do, however, regard Moll as *femina economica*, Defoe's treatment of her experience need not be seen as either an indictment of capitalism or a broader condemnation of human materialism in general. Instead, the novel would seem to be, among other things, an examination of just what money has come to mean to civilized man. And therein lies the irony.

At this point in the argument, it is important to remember that what we may be tempted to see as Moll's propensity for hard-headed, rational calculation is actually motivated by her fears for her own survival, her desire to rise above her low origins. The irony of her situation is exactly that which Brown recognizes in Horace: he "sees poetry as a career, like all careers (trader, soldier, athlete, etc.) basically characterized by self-sacrifice and instinctual renunciation; it is nevertheless worth while if success will enable him 'to strike the stars with head sublime.'" But, says Brown, Horace's expressed hope that he "shall not altogether die" is "the hope of the man who has not lived, whose life has been spent conquering death." Horace's dedication to his work, to his "royal accumulation," has been ironically at once "death-defying and deadening." If Moll has, as so many critics argue, betrayed her higher self, become subhuman in that she is a kind of money-making machine, the irony is that she has achieved that unhappy result in the effort to achieve its opposite—the effort, that is, to become superhuman.

The sacrificial nature of her dedication becomes especially clear in her erotic response to money. Van Ghent was among the first to point to the sexual suggestiveness implicit in Moll's financial transactions with her Bath gentleman:

> reaching in his Pocket, [he] pull'd out a Key, and bad me open a little Walnut-tree box he had upon the Table, and bring him such a Drawer, which I did, in which Drawer there was a great deal of Money in Gold, I believe near 200 Guineas, but I knew not how much: He took the Drawer, and taking my hand, made me put it in, and take a whole handful; I was backward at that, but he held my Hand hard in his Hand, and put it into the Drawer, and made me take out as many Guineas almost as I could well take up at once.
>
> When I had done so, he made me put them into my Lap.

We have earlier encountered an anticipation of this kind of thing when Moll's Colchester lover presents her with "a silk Purse, with an Hundred Guineas in it." "My Colour," Moll tells us, "came and went, at the Sight of the Purse, and with the fire of his Proposal together; so that I could not say a Word, and he easily perceiv'd it; so putting the Purse into my Bosom, I made no more Resistance to him." And in the scene at the gambling house late in the novel, Moll's handling of the money belonging to "the gentle-man who had the Box" possesses a similar suggestiveness: "He . . . made me take the Box, which was a bold Venture: However, I held the Box so long that I had gain'd him his whole Money, and had a handful of Guineas in my Lap. . . . I understood the Game well enough, tho' I pretended I did not, and play'd cautiously; it was to keep a good Stock in my Lap, out of which I every now and then convey'd some into my Pocket; but in such a manner . . . as I was sure he cou'd not see it."

This is the game Moll has been playing all her life. For Moll, accumulating stock is tantamount to accumulating life, and thus she characterizes her "spending upon the main Stock," to which she is at one point reduced, as "but a certain kind of *bleeding to Death*." We hear the same phrase again when she reaches another low point in her career: "I LIV'D Two Years in this dismal Condition wasting that little I had, weeping continually over my dismal Circumstances, and as it were only bleeding to Death, without the least hope or prospect of help from God or Man; and now I had cried so long, and so often, that Tears were . . . exhausted, and I began to be Desperate, for I grew Poor apace."

There is, apropos of this, a notable irony in the nature of many of the things Moll steals, symbolically associated as they are with fertility: baby clothes, for example, and wedding rings and a horse (which, to add to the irony, she does not know what to do with once she has it). At one point too she steals from a pregnant woman.

Moll is well aware that, as Brown puts it, "money *breeds*," and it is her desire, with reference to any money she has in hand, that "the Interest of it maintain me." In effect, she prefers devoting her reproductive capacities to producing money rather than children. Gold is the beloved offspring of her labor.

Understandably, then, Moll is always as concerned to have any children she produces "taken happily off of my Hands," as she is to retain any money she accrues "in my own Hands." And she sees to it that any of her children who are unhappily left on her hands will be as little expense as possible. The only child of hers of whom we hear in some detail is the son in Virginia, who proves to have become "a handsome comely young Gentleman in flourishing Circumstances," and hence an interest-bearing investment of time and energy. Just as Moll values her land—"very fertile and good"—in Virginia because it produces crops that produce income, so she values her own productiveness only if the product in turn reproduces satisfactorily. She speaks toward the end of her story of going "over the Bay to see my son and to receive another Year's Income of my Plantation." And she describes her son in this scene as "the same kind dutiful and obliging Creature as ever," and tells us that he "treated me now at his own House, paid me my hundred Pound, and sent me Home again loaded with Presents."

At this juncture it may seem that we have slipped back into something resembling the familiar ironic reading of Moll's "adventures." But a point that psychologist Ernest Becker makes, in explicating Norman Brown, may provide a helpful clarification: "If we say that 'money is God,' this seems like a simple and cynical observation on the corruptibility of men. But if we say that 'money negotiates immortality and therefore is God,' this is a scientific formula that is limpidly objective to any serious student of man." In these terms, the point being argued here is that in *Moll Flanders* Defoe emerges as "a serious student of man" and is not, as has so often been suggested, making "a simple and cynical observation on the corruptibility of men."

Moll, in these terms, remains always an upward aspirer. What Van Ghent calls "the spiritual dimension" is, in fact, present. The distinction between the sacred and the profane does not, in this context, exist. Perhaps a brief consideration of Moll's preoccupation not simply with money but with gold will clarify the point still further. The "prize" that she defines as her "greatest" consists of "a Gold Chain, an old fashion'd thing, the Locket of which was broken, so that I suppose it had not been us'd some Years, but the Gold was not the worse for that; also a little Box of burying Rings, the Lady's Wedding-Ring, and some broken bits of old Lockets of Gold, a Gold watch, and a Purse with about 24£ value in old pieces of Gold Coin." But by this time we have already heard a great deal from Moll about gold watches, gold rings, and gold coins—including those coins belonging to the Bath gentleman that she sifts so lovingly through her fingers—and Jemy's possessions—"ten Guineas, his Gold Watch, and two little Rings, one a small Diamond Ring, worth only about six Pound, and the other a plain Gold Ring"—which, she tells us, she "Sat . . . down and look'd upon . . . two Hours together." Gold, Becker observes, is associated with both the fire god Agni and the sun's disc. "Money," he goes on, "sums up the *causa sui* project all in itself: how man, with the tremendous ingenuity of his mind and the materials of his earth can contrive the dazzling glitter, the magical ratios, the purchase of other men and their labors, to link his destiny with the stars and live down his animal body."

It is not, then, that Moll worships and hence serves money, unless we say that here again it is a case of her serving in order to be served, for in her view the money she possesses serves her—serves, that is, to raise her above the lowly state into which she was born. One might say that she works religiously toward that end. Her career, Defoe tells us in his preface, is "fruitful of Instruction" that "no Case can be so low, so despicable, or so empty of Prospect, but that an unwearied Industry will go a great way to deliver us from it, will in time raise the meanest Creature to appear again in the World, and give him a new Cast for his Life." Money brings deliverance. And Moll can feel godlike in her powers of reproduction, contemplating fondly the fruits of her labors. The irony lies in Defoe's phrase *unwearied Industry,* since we see here again a situation that can only be regarded as a sacrificing of self to the end of self-perpetuation. If Moll is a self-made woman, she is so at the expense of her own energies, her own life force.

The fact is, moreover, that Moll is never truly able to go it alone; she is never able to rise above her state of dependency. Even more persistently than Crusoe's, her feelings of powerlessness and her need for protection continue to make themselves felt. She may at times believe that money is, as she tells Jemy in Newgate, "the only Friend in such a Condition," the only means of escape from servitude, but over and over she admits to the need for other friends as well: "to be Friendless," she says, "is the worst Condition, next to being in want, that a Woman can be reduc'd to." For Moll, friendlessness and exposure are virtually synonymous, just as are poverty and exposure. She characterizes herself in her childhood as "a poor desolate Girl without Friends, without Cloaths, without Help or Helper" and hence "expos'd to very great Distresses," and at the time when she is faced with losing her Colchester lover, she imagines "being turn'd out to the wide World, a meer cast off Whore . . . and perhaps expos'd as such; with little to provide for myself; with no Friend, no Acquaintance in the whole World, out of that Town." "To have friends, is power," says Hobbes.

It is true that Moll has, as noted earlier, a great deal to say about the tendency of women not to take due precautions in the matter of husband-choosing: "'Tis nothing," she declares, "but lack of Courage, the fear of not being Marry'd at all, and of that frightful State of Life called *an Old Maid.*" But she is by no means advocating the single state, and she goes on, "would the Ladies once but get above that Fear, and manage rightly, they would more certainly avoid it by standing their Ground, in a Case so absolutely Necessary to their Felicity than by exposing themselves as they do; and if they did not Marry so soon as they may do otherwise, they would make themselves amends by Marrying safer."

Despite all of Moll's own ingenious machinations and painstaking precautions, however, she finds herself more than once exposed—left in a "dismal and disconsolate Case," "left perfectly Friendless and Helpless." After her return from Virginia, she complains of being "entirely without Friends, nay, even so much as without Acquaintance." And after the death of her banker husband, she says unhappily, "I had no Assistant, no Friend to comfort or advise me," and goes on to warn, "O let none read this part without seriously reflecting on the Circumstances of a desolate State, and how they would grapple with meer want of Friends and want of Bread." In Newgate, she cries, "Lord! what will become of me, I shall be cast to be sure, and there is nothing beyond that but Death! I have no Friends, what shall I do?" And finally, faced with crossing Chesapeake Bay some years later, she fears being "left naked and destitute, and in a wild, strange Place, not having one Friend or Acquaintance in all that part of the World." And she adds, "The very thought of it gives me some horror, even since the Danger is past."

Moll's fears of being "left alone in the World to shift for myself" are never allayed. Always she looks to her lovers and her husbands for protection. From the time she learns that the mother of the Colchester family is threatening "to turn me out-of-Doors" and finds reassurance in her lover's promise that "he would Protect me from all the World," she finds that world a terrifying place to face alone.

Moll's world, of course, is scarcely ever the natural one with which Robinson Crusoe must deal. But what little natural imagery she uses suggests that she too regards nature as unfriendly. "I saw the cloud, tho' I did not foresee the Storm" she says of her experience with her Colchester lover. And when she has managed to secure her banker husband, she remarks, "I seem'd landed in a safe Harbour after the Stormy Voyage of Life was at an end."

And in some ways Moll's actual experiences of the natural world do resemble Crusoe's. She often sets out on sea voyages that prove to be "long and full of Dangers," after which she comes at last "safe to the Coast." Moll's voyages, while not exploratory and expansive in the same sense as Crusoe's, are undeniably expansive in another sense. She usually ventures forth onto the water when the land has become inhospitable. She undertakes her first trip to Virginia, for example—"a terrible passage," during which she and her husband are "frighted twice with dreadful Storms"— only when she finds herself with little cash in hand and when her husband has told her that he owns "a very good house there, well furnished." It is true that so long as she has "Possession" of "a House well furnished and a Husband in very good Circumstances," her fears remain largely in abeyance and she stays where she is. She feels momentarily protected and provided for.

But she can never be "easy" for long. There *are* times when God, or Providence, is on her side. This she finds, though, is not always the case. When, she says of her Bath lover, he "abandon'd me and refus'd to see me any more," it was because he was "struck by the hand of God." And she is left as if "abandon'd by heaven." And she tells us that after living "in an uninterrupted course of Ease and Content for Five Years" with her banker husband, "a sudden Blow from an almost invisible Hand, blasted all my Happiness, and turn'd me out into the World in a Condition the reverse of all that had been before it." The fear of abandonment haunts Moll all her life.

There is, in this connection, a telling passage about midway through the book, in which Moll holds forth at some length on the helplessness of children:

> It is manifest to all that understand anything of Children, that we are born into the World helpless and uncapable, either to supply our own Wants, or so much as make them known; and that without help we must Perish; and this help requires not only an assisting Hand, whether of the Mother or some Body else; but there are two Things necessary in that assisting Hand, that is, Care and Skill; without both which, half the Children that are born would die; nay, tho' they were not to be deny'd Food; and one half more of those that remain'd would be Cripples or Fools, loose their Limbs, and perhaps their Sense: I Question not but that these are partly the Reasons why Affection was plac'd by Nature in the Hearts of Mothers to their Children; without which they would never be able to give themselves up, as 'tis necessary they should, to the Care and waking Pains needful to the Support of their Children.
>
> Since this Care is needful to the Life of Children, to neglect them is to Murther them; again to give them up to be Manag'd by those People, who have none of that needful Affection, plac'd by Nature in them, is to Neglect them in the highest Degree; nay, in some it goes farther, and is a Neglect in order to their being Lost; so that 'tis an intentional Murther, whether the Child lives or dies.

Supposedly, Moll's concern here is with the fate of her own child. Yet it seems evident, from the ensuing paragraph, that she herself is, in her own mind, that helpless child whose welfare concerns her so deeply, for there she refers to "my Governess, who I had now learn'd to call Mother" and relates: "She ask'd me if she had not been Careful, and Tender of me in my Lying-In, as if I had been her own Child?" In fact, if all the men in Moll's life are essentially father-figures, most of the women are just as clearly mother-figures. The first—her "good old Nurse, Mother, I ought rather to call her," who "bred up the Children" in her school "with a great deal of Art, as well as with a great deal of Care"—is only one of a long series of women who look after Moll with "Care and Skill." There is her own mother in Virginia; there is "Mother Midnight," who arranges so competently for one of Moll's many lyings-in and who thereafter calls her "Child" and acts "a true Mother to [her]" until the transport ship leaves for Virginia. All these women are nurturers and comforters; all provide homes ("I came Home to my Governess," says Moll more than once after a thieving foray); and all give her instruction in the way she should go in the interest of her own prosperity.

Moll may "reign" supreme in the kingdom of London thieves, but she needs authority figures nonetheless—friends and mothers to advise and direct her. "I was now a loose unguided Creature," she says of herself at forty-two, "and had no Help, no Assistance, no Guide for my Conduct." And we may remember that she goes on to lament, "I had not one Friend in the World with whom to trust that little I had, or to direct me how to dispose of it." And at an earlier stage of her career, she has told her "Dear and faithful Friend, the Captain's Wife" that "I would give up myself wholly to her Directions, and that I would have neither Tongue to speak, or Feet to step in that Affair, but as she should direct me; depending that she would Extricate me out of every Difficulty that she brought me into." Clearly, Moll follows Hobbes in taking a wholly practical view of the mother-child relationship.

Whatever her successes, Moll remains always a child in need of a governess. Adept though she is at the power game, she continues to experience herself as powerless. Thus she comments, in recounting her actions after successfully making off with a silver tankard: "I came Home to my Governess, and now I thought it was a time to try her, that if I might be put to the Necessity of being expos'd, she might offer me some assistance." And thus we hear her, toward the end of her narrative, recalling her need to secure from her mother in Virginia her means of independence from her brother/husband: "for my Mother had promis'd me very solemnly, that when she died, she would do something for me, and leave it so, as that, if I was Living, I should one way or other come at it, without its being in the Power of her Son, *my brother and Husband* to prevent it."

Her sense of powerlessness is compounded by her awareness that she can never fully depend on the people on whom she depends. Maximillian Novak reminds us that the word *mother* is usually applied to the Madam of a brothel. It seems that Moll must depend for protection on a fellow human being who is as inspired by the profit motive as she is herself and whose "children" are her source of income. Moll knows, of course, that all people live at the expense of other people, and at the time of the arrest of a fellow thief, she compliments herself on the canniness she possesses that has been born of that knowledge: "Here again my old Caution stood me in good stead; . . . I kept close a great while upon the Occasion of this Womans disaster; I knew that if I should do any thing that should Miscarry, and should be carried to Prison she would be there, and ready to Witness against me, and perhaps save her Life at my Expence." What Moll does is to save her own life at the expense of "this poor Woman"—a fact which, as she says, "troubl'd me exceedingly." But, she continues, "my own Life, which was so evidently in Danger, took off all my tenderness; and seeing she was not put to Death, I was easy at her Transportation, because she was then out of the way of doing me any Mischief." And "tenderness" has not even been a problem in the case of another of her fellow thieves who winds up in Newgate. Fearing that he "might . . . have bought his own Life at the Expence of mine," Moll expresses heartfelt relief at "the joyful News that he was hang'd, which was the best News to me that I had heard a great while." For Moll, a condition of "dreadful Exigence" justifies anything; and she assumes that everyone else holds the same view—hence her distrust of the foster parents her governess proposes for her child. Even though she acknowledges that they "want neither Care nor Skill," she still protests: "now we know Mother . . . that those are poor People, and their Gain consists in being quit of the Charge as soon as they can; how can I doubt but that, as it is best for them to have the Child die, they are not over Solicitous about its Life?" But the governess has an answer ready that largely satisfies her: "I tell you their Credit depends upon the Child's Life, and they are as careful as any Mother of you all."

What Moll says she wants for her child—that it "be carefully look'd after and have Justice done it"—is what, in reality, she desperately wants for herself and yet trusts no one to provide. Rather, she is certain that even her friends will, if they can, live at her expense. Whatever Moll may say about trustworthy friends, "dear and faithful" friends, the predatory nature of her world is not to be gainsaid. She always, therefore, holds something back, never giving herself completely to anyone. Just as she withholds from Jemy a complete accounting of her assets—being "resolved . . . to keep what I had left . . . in Reserve," so she withholds from him a considerable stock of information about herself. When, for example, she first learns the truth about Jemy, she comments, "It was my happiness hitherto that I had not discovered myself, or my Circumstances at all; no not so much as my

Name; and seeing there was nothing to be expected from him, however good Humoured, and however honest he seem'd to be, but to live on what I knew would soon be wasted, I resolv'd to conceal everything, but the *Bank Bill,* and the Eleven Guineas." At the time of their first parting, moreover, she tells us, "I Gave him a Direction how to write to me, tho' still I reserv'd the grand Secret . . . which was not to let him know my true Name, who I was, or where to be found." And when, many years later, she has come to Virginia with him, she notes, "I could never so much as think of breaking the Secret of my former Marriage to my new Husband; It was not a Story, as I thought would bear telling, nor could I tell what might be the Consequences of it." She practices a similar reserve with the other person in her life in whom she professes to feel the greatest confidence, namely, Mother Midnight. At one point she indicates she is "frighted" at the thought that her governess knows more than she should about her past: "but reflecting that it cou'd not be possible for her to know anything about me, that Disorder went off, and I began to be easie, but it was not presently."

Here again what Moll fears is exposure. To tell anyone the real truth about oneself is a dangerous practice, and only "horrible Apprehensions" ever drive Moll to it. Such is the case when she is hiding out after her fellow thief has been sent to Newgate. "I had no Recourse, no Friend, no Confident but my old Governess," she says, "and I knew no Remedy but to put my Life into her Hands, and so I did, for I let her know where to send to me." On an earlier occasion, however, she has taken care *not* to let this same friend know her whereabouts. Having declared that there was "no concealing any thing from her," she nonetheless concludes, as she contemplates a journey to West Chester, "at last it came as an Addition to my Design of going into the Country that it would be an excellent Blind to my old Governess, and would cover all my other affairs."

From the time Moll, as a little girl, hides herself from the gypsies, she has been adept at concealment; and late in her story she remarks, "let them say what they please of our Sex not being able to keep a Secret; my Life is a plain Conviction to me of the Contrary." But she then goes on to add that "a Secret of Moment should always have a Confident, a bosom Friend, to whom we may Communicate the Joy of it, or the Grief of it." She regards confiding her secrets to a friend as a kind of safety valve.

Moll's "account" of her life is, in fact, itself a kind of confession—a disclosure of secrets she might otherwise find oppressive. Yet as with the "relief" she gains from letting Jemy in on as much of her past as she thinks is necessary, she is, one supposes, telling us only as much as she must in order to gain relief from "the Oppression of this weight." Certainly, she does withhold information from her readers. If most of the people in her life do not know who she really is, neither do her readers ever really know. To tell us would be to take a chance on giving too much away. As her governess says to her in another context, "you would be Conceal'd and Discover'd both together."

Chronology

1660	Daniel Foe born in London to a fairly prosperous tallow chandler, James Foe, and his wife, Alice.
1662	Family follows their pastor, Dr. Samuel Annesley, out of the Church of England because of the Act of Uniformity; they are now Presbyterians.
ca. 1668	Mother dies.
ca. 1671–79	Studies at the Reverend James Fisher's school at Dorking, Surrey; then, Oxford and Cambridge being closed to Dissenters, attends the Reverend Charles Morton's school at Newington Green. Foe's education, although preparing him for the ministry, includes science and is broader than studies at the universities.
1683	Merchant in the import/export business in Freeman's Yard, Cornhill (London). Publishes first political tract; no copy is known.
1684	Marries Mary Tuffley, daughter of a prosperous Dissenting wine-cooper. She bears him eight children, six of whom survive.
1685–92	Prospers in business: trades in hosiery, imports wine and tobacco, insures ships. Travels in England and on the Continent for business. Publishes political tracts.
1685	Joins the Protestant Duke of Monmouth's rebellion against Catholic James II; manages to escape after the disastrous Battle of Sedgemoor.
1688–1702	Supports William III, serving him in various offices.
1688	Admitted to the Butcher's Company, a guild. Publishes his first extant political tract against James II. Rides to Henley to join the advancing forces of William III.

133

1690–91	Contributes to the *Athenian Mercury;* belongs to the Athenian Society.
1692	Declares bankruptcy, a result of rash speculations and losses in his ship insurance caused by the war with France. Within ten years, pays back all but £5,000, but is never again quite clear of debt.
1695	When manager-trustee of the royal lotteries, changes his name to "De Foe."
1697	Publishes *An Essay upon Projects,* which attracts politicians' attention.
1701	Publishes *The True-Born Englishman: A Satyr,* a poetic defense of William III's Dutch ancestry. Youngest child, Sophia, baptized.
1702	William III dies; Anne's accession ends Defoe's hopes of preferment. The rise of the Tories increases pressure on the Dissenters. Defoe writes *The Shortest Way with the Dissenters: or Proposals For The Establishment of The Church,* an ironic attack on the intolerance of the High Church.
1703	Accused of seditions libel, Defoe is arrested for writing *The Shortest Way.* Fined, sent to Newgate, sentenced to stand in the pillory. Writes *Hymn to the Pillory.* Second bankruptcy. Appeals to the Tory minister Harley, who secures his release and employs him. Publishes an authorized edition of his collected works.
1703–14	Pamphleteer and intelligence agent for Harley.
1704–13	Writes and edits *The Review* (a weekly, later triweekly), the main government organ (moderate Tory), in which Defoe discusses current affairs, politics, religion, trade, and manners and morals. The paper influences both later essay periodicals and the newspaper press.
1706–10	As government secret agent, travels frequently in Scotland to promote the Act of Union.
1708	Moves to Stoke Newington, suburb north of London, where he lives the rest of his life.
1713–14	Repeatedly arrested by Harley's political enemies, once for publishing ironical tracts in support of the Hanoverian succession.
1715	Publishes *The Family Instructor,* a conduct manual, his most popular didactic work.

1715–30	Undertakes propaganda and intelligence work for successive Whig ministries after Harley's fall.
1718	Publishes the second volume of *The Family Instructor*.
1719	*The Life and Strange Surprising Adventures of Robinson Crusoe of York, Mariner* and *The Farther Adventures of Robinson Crusoe*.
1720	*Memoirs of a Cavalier; The Life, Adventures, and Pyracies of the Famous Captain Singleton*.
1722	*The Fortunes and Misfortunes of the Famous Moll Flanders, A Journal of the Plague Year*, and *The History and Remarkable Life of the Truly Honourable Colonel Jacque, Commonly Call'd Colonel Jack*.
1724	*The Fortunate Mistress: Or . . . Roxana*.
1724–26	*A Tour Thro' the Whole Island of Great Britain* (three volumes).
1725	*The Complete English Tradesman* and pirate and criminal "lives."
1726	*The Political History of the Devil*.
1727	*Conjugal Lewdness (A Treatise Concerning the Use and Abuse of the Marriage Bed), An Essay on the History and Reality of Apparitions, A New Family Instructor*, and a second volume of *The Complete English Tradesman*.
1728	"Augusta Triumphans: Or, The Way To Make London The most flourishing city in the Universe" and *A Plan of the English Commerce*.
1731	Dies of a "lethargy" in Ropemaker's Alley (London), hiding from creditors. Buried in Bunhill Fields along with John Bunyan and other Puritans.

Contributors

HAROLD BLOOM, Sterling Professor of the Humanities at Yale University, is the author of *The Anxiety of Influence, Poetry and Repression,* and many other volumes of literary criticism. His forthcoming study, *Freud: Transference and Authority,* attempts a full-scale reading of all of Freud's major writings. A MacArthur Prize Fellow, he is general editor of five series of literary criticism published by Chelsea House. During 1987–88, he was appointed Charles Eliot Norton Professor of Poetry at Harvard University.

MARTIN PRICE is Sterling Professor of English at Yale University. His books include *Swift's Rhetorical Art: A Study in Structure and Meaning, To the Palace of Wisdom: Studies in Order and Energy from Dryden to Blake,* and a number of edited volumes on the literature of the seventeenth, eighteenth, and nineteenth centuries.

JOHN J. RICHETTI is Professor of English at Rutgers University. He is the author of *Popular Fiction Before Richardson: Narrative Patterns 1700–1739* and *Defoe's Narratives: Situations and Structures.*

MIRIAM LERENBAUM is a member of the English Department at the State University of New York, Binghamton, and the author of *Alexander Pope's Magnum Opus: 1727–1744.*

MAXIMILLIAN E. NOVAK is Professor of English at the University of California, Los Angeles. His numerous works include *Realism, Myth, and History in Defoe's Fiction.*

MICHAEL M. BOARDMAN, Associate Professor of English at Tulane University, is the author of *Defoe and the Uses of Narrative.*

IAN A. BELL teaches in the English Department of the University College of Wales, Aberystwyth, and has recently published *Defoe's Fiction.*

VIRGINIA OGDEN BIRDSALL teaches in the English Department at the University of Connecticut and is the author of *Defoe's Perpetual Seekers: A Study of the Major Fiction*.

Bibliography

Alkon, Paul K. *Defoe and Fictional Time*. Athens: University of Georgia Press, 1979.

Alter, Robert. *Rogue's Progress: Studies in the Picaresque Novel*. Cambridge: Harvard University Press, 1964.

Backscheider, Paula R. *Daniel Defoe: Ambition and Innovation*. Lexington: Kentucky University Press, 1987.

Baine, Rodney M. *Daniel Defoe and the Supernatural*. Athens: University of Georgia Press, 1968.

Birdsall, Virginia Ogden. "Moll Flanders' First Love." *Papers of the Michigan Academy of Science, Arts, and Letters* 46 (1961): 635–43.

Bjornson, Richard. *The Picaresque Hero in European Fiction*. Madison: University of Wisconsin Press, 1977.

Booth, Wayne C. *The Rhetoric of Fiction*. Chicago: University of Chicago Press, 1961.

Brooks, Douglas. "Moll Flanders." *Essays in Criticism* 19 (1969): 46–59.

Byrd, Max, ed. *Daniel Defoe: A Collection of Critical Essays*. Englewood Cliffs, N.J.: Prentice-Hall, 1976.

Dobree, Bonamy. *English Literature in the Early Eighteenth Century*. Oxford: Clarendon, 1959.

Donoghue, Denis. "The Values of *Moll Flanders.*" *Sewanee Review* 71 (1963): 287–303.

Donovan, Robert Alan. *The Shaping Vision: Imagination in the English Novel from Defoe to Dickens*. Ithaca, N.Y.: Cornell University Press, 1966.

Dottin, Paul. *The Life and Strange Surprizing Adventures of Daniel Defoe*. New York: Macauly, 1929.

Earle, Peter. *The World of Defoe*. London: Weidenfeld & Nicolson, 1976.

Elliott, Robert C. *Twentieth-Century Interpretations of* Moll Flanders: *A Collection of Critical Essays*. Englewood Cliffs, N.J.: Prentice-Hall, 1970.

Erickson, Robert A. "Moll's Fate: 'Mother Midnight' and *Moll Flanders.*" *Studies in Philology* 76 (1979): 75–100.

Goldberg, M. A. "*Moll Flanders:* Christian Allegory in a Hobbesian Mode." *University Review* 33 (1967): 267–78.

Hartog, Curt. "Aggression, Femininity and Irony in *Moll Flanders.*" *Literature and Psychology* 22 (1972): 121–38.

James, E. Anthony. *Daniel Defoe's Many Voices*. Amsterdam: Rodopi, 1972.

Karl, Frederick R. "Moll's Many-Colored Coat: Veil and Disguise in the Fiction of Defoe." *Studies in the Novel* 5 (1973): 86–97.

Koonce, H. L. "Moll's Muddle: Defoe's Use of Irony in *Moll Flanders*." *ELH* 30 (1963): 377–94.

Lukács, Georg. *The Historical Novel*. Translated by Hannah and Stanley Mitchell. Lincoln: University of Nebraska Press, 1983.

McVeagh, John. "Rochester and Defoe: A Study in Influence." *Studies in English Literature* 14 (1974): 327–41.

Moore, John Robert. *Daniel Defoe: Citizen of the Modern World*. Chicago: University of Chicago Press, 1958.

Novak, Maximillian E. "The Problem of Necessity in Defoe's Fiction." *Philological Quarterly* 40 (1961): 513–24.

————. *Defoe and the Nature of Man*. Oxford: Oxford University Press, 1963.

————. "Defoe's Theory of Fiction." *Studies in Philology* 61 (1964): 650–68.

Rogers, Pat, ed. *Defoe: The Critical Heritage*. London: Routledge & Kegan Paul, 1972.

Ross, John F. *Swift and Defoe: A Study in Relationship*. University of California Publication in English 11. Berkeley and Los Angeles: University of California Press, 1941.

Secord, Arther W. *Studies in the Narrative Method of Defoe*. 1924. Reprint. New York: Russell & Russell, 1963.

Sherbo, Arthur. "Moll's Friends." In *Studies in the Eighteenth Century English Novel*, edited by Arthur Sherbo. East Lansing: Michigan State University Press, 1969.

Starr, G. A. *Defoe and Casuistry*. Princeton, N.J.: Princeton University Press, 1971.

Stephen, Leslie. "Defoe's Novels." In *Hours in a Library*. 3 vols. 2d ed. London: Smith, Elder, 1892.

Sutherland, James. *Daniel Defoe: A Critical Study*. Cambridge: Harvard University Press, 1971.

————. *Defoe*. Philadelphia: Lippincott, 1938.

Van Ghent, Dorothy. *The English Novel: Form and Function*. New York: Holt, Rinehart & Winston, 1953.

Walton, James. "The Romance of Gentility: Defoe's Heroes and Heroines." *Literary Monographs* 4 (1971): 89–135.

Watt, Ian. *The Rise of the English Novel*. Berkeley and Los Angeles: University of California Press, 1957.

————. "The Recent Critical Fortunes of Moll Flanders." *Eighteenth-Century Studies* 1 (1967): 109–26.

Wilson, Walter. *Memoirs of the Life and Times of Daniel Defoe*. 3 vols. 1830. Reprint. New York: AMS, 1973.

Woolf, Virginia. "Defoe." In *The Common Reader*. New York: Harcourt, Brace & World, 1925.

Zimmerman, Everett. *Defoe and the Novel*. Berkeley and Los Angeles: University of California Press, 1975.

Acknowledgments

"The Divided Heart" by Martin Price from *To the Palace of Wisdom: Studies in Order and Energy from Dryden to Blake* by Martin Price, © 1964 by Martin Price. Reprinted by permission of the author and Southern Illinois University Press.

"The Dialectic of Power" (originally entitled "*Moll Flanders*: The Dialectic of Power") by John J. Richetti from *Defoe's Narratives: Situations and Structures* by John J. Richetti, © 1975 by Oxford University Press. Reprinted by permission.

"A Woman on Her Own Account" (originally entitled "*Moll Flanders*: A Woman on Her Own Account") by Miriam Lerenbaum from *The Authority of Experience: Essays in Feminist Criticism,* edited by Arlyn Diamond and Lee R. Edwards, © 1977 by the University of Massachusetts Press. Reprinted by permission of the University of Massachusetts Press.

"Openness and Complexity in *Moll Flanders*" (originally entitled "'Unweary'd Traveller' and 'Indifferent Monitor': Openness and Complexity in *Moll Flanders*") by Maximillian E. Novak from *Realism, Myth, and History in Defoe's Fiction* by Maximillian E. Novak, © 1983 by the University of Nebraska Press. Reprinted by permission of the University of Nebraska Press.

"Moll Flanders: Inside and Out" by Michael M. Boardman from *Defoe and the Uses of Narrative* by Michael M. Boardman, © 1983 by Rutgers, the State University of New Jersey. Reprinted by permission.

"Crime and Comfort" (originally entitled "*Moll Flanders*: Crime and Comfort") by Ian A. Bell from *Defoe's Fiction* by Ian A. Bell, © 1985 by Ian A. Bell. Reprinted by permission of Croom Helm Ltd.

"Out of the Jaws of Destruction" (originally entitled "*Moll Flanders*: 'Out of the Jaws of Destruction'") by Virginia Ogden Birdsall from *Defoe's Perpetual Seekers: A Study of the Major Fiction* by Virginia Ogden Birdsall, © 1985 by Associated University Presses, Inc. Reprinted by permission of Associated University Presses, Inc.

Index